FROM WORTHLESS TO WORTHY

The God Help Me series

From Worry to Worship
A 30-Day Devotional Guide

From Worthless to Worthy
A 30-Day Guide to Overcoming Inferiority

FROM WORTHLESS TO

Worthy

A 30-DAY GUIDE
TO OVERCOMING
INFERIORITY

JULIE MORRIS

new
hope
PUBLISHERS

Birmingham, Alabama

New Hope® Publishers
P. O. Box 12065
Birmingham, AL 35202-2065
www.newhopepubl.com

Library of Congress Cataloging-in-Publication Data
Morris, Julie.
From worthless to worthy : a 30-day guide to overcoming inferiority / Julie Morris.
p. cm.— (God help me series)
ISBN 1-56309-771-0
1. Self-esteem-Religious aspects-Christianity. 2. Devotional calendars. I. Title.
BV4647.S43M67 2004
242'.4—dc22
2004005126

ISBN: 1-56309-771-0
N044101 • 0604 • 5M1

Acknowledgments

I would like to thank Ricci Waters, my life-long friend, Sarah Morris, my precious daughter, and Sue Mackle, my faithful accountability partner, for the help and encouragement they gave me while I wrote *From Worthless to Worthy*.

Table of Contents

Introduction

"Please, oh please pick me!" There were only two of us left—me and another girl, named Carol—and I couldn't bear to be the last one chosen…again. My unspoken plea went unnoticed, though. The popular kid in charge of choosing up sides for our sixth grade ball team said with contempt, "If I have to choose one of them, I'll take Carol."

Something was the matter with me. I didn't make mistakes—I was a mistake. I couldn't do anything right. I felt stupid, unattractive and just plain worthless. Although eventually I earned two college degrees and gained a precious husband and two adorable children, these feelings of inferiority and shame continued to haunt me.

When I became a Christian, it was impossible for me to believe the gospel message that God loved me just the way I was. I felt that I had to perform for God and try to make Him like me, so I could like myself. I also felt that I had to perform for others so that they would like me, too.

When I made mistakes I beat myself up unmercifully, telling myself that I was hopeless and that I would never change. I read Bible verses about God's unconditional love for me, and even taught them to others, but I couldn't stop feeling ashamed of myself.

Slowly, over the years, God began showing me practical ways to let go of the lies I believed about myself. I learned how to see myself through His eyes and stop looking to my own accomplishments or the approval of others for my sense of worth. I found that by spending just a few minutes with the Lord every morning I could make amazing progress in shedding my feelings of inferiority and the lifestyle that went with them.

I am thrilled to share these things with you so that you can get rid of your feelings of inferiority like I did. As you spend a few minutes a day reading this book and doing the short exercises, I pray that you will understand how precious you are to God—that you are unique, created with a purpose and a plan. I pray that you will understand that when you surrender your life to the Lord—no matter what kind of mess it is in—God can use your weaknesses, your mistakes, and even your past sins for your good and His glory. And I pray that you will experience the Lord's unconditional love and forgiveness, through Christ, like you never have before—that deep within your spirit you will find a new confidence and a new hope. I know, from experience, that when this happens, an exciting transformation takes place: **You will finally be free to become the person you have always wanted to be.**

Spend 15 Minutes a Day

I have designed this book so that you can make exciting progress in getting free of inferiority feelings by spending just 15 minutes a day for 30 days. I will give you biblical insights, thought-provoking questions, and practical suggestions that will help you to draw closer to Christ and let Him give you a feeling of worth.

As you read, make lots of notes in your book and answer the questions thoughtfully. Draw stars in the margins to remind yourself of practical suggestions that you want to try. Choose a few to start practicing right away. Later, reread what you starred and try other new things.

Daily sections

Each daily section includes the following parts that you can easily complete in 15 minutes:

• **Read About It**—my meditation on a verse that has helped me to overcome feelings of inferiority.

(The person God has always wanted you to be.)

• **Think About It**—practical information that will encourage you to apply that day's Bible verse to your own life.

• **Write About It**—a questionnaire that will help you to get to the roots of your feelings of inferiority and replace them with confidence in Christ.

• **Pray About It**—a place for you to write a prayer about the Scripture and questionnaire. This section also includes my prayer reflecting back on the focus of the day.

• **Do It**—a helpful suggestion that will encourage you to put the principles taught that day into action.

Group Study Guide

At the end of the book I have included a brief Leader's Guide so that you may use *From Worthless to Worthy* in a group setting—in Bible studies, support groups, or Sunday school classes. You can also start a group in your neighborhood or with another friend or two. The Leader's Guide offers questions that focus on five daily sections a week, for a total of six weeks. These questions will encourage you to grow spiritually, share honestly, and find support and encouragement from other Christians.

Julie Morris would love to hear from you! Her address is:

5184 Caldwell Mill Road,
Suite 204, Box 266,
Hoover, AL 35244
or julie@guidedbyhim.com

For additional resources and information about Julie's seminars and retreats, check out her Websites at:
www.worthlesstoworthy.com
www.worrytoworship.com
www.stepforwarddiet.com

Chapter 1

How Can I Accept God's Love for Me the Way I Am?

Day 1
Experiencing God's Mercy

Today's Verse

Titus 3:5 *(NLT)— "He saved us, not because of the good things we did, but because of his mercy."*

Read About It

"You're stupid!" "You're fat!" "You're lazy!" Everywhere I turned while I was growing up someone was putting a different label on me, and they penetrated deep into my soul, leaving me with scars far more disfiguring than ones that are just skin deep.

Sticks and stones can break your bones, but names can hurt far worse.

When I was about nine years old, I remember writing a list of everything I hated about myself—about 20 items. I took my list to my mother and when I showed it to her, tears filled her eyes. She hugged me and told me to write a list of all of the good things about myself. But hard as I tried, I couldn't think of one. I didn't like anything about myself, and even though my mother did everything she could to help me to overcome my feelings of worthlessness, I spent the next 30 years feeling ashamed and hopeless, striving to please people because I believed the lie that if people liked me, I would finally like myself.

When I became a Christian, I added God to the list of those I needed to please. I worked hard to deserve His love because I was sure that every time I sinned, God got disgusted with me and was sorry that He was my Father. I was also sure that after I had sinned just one too many times, He would give up on me completely, kick me out of His family, and refuse to let me into heaven. I reasoned that if I did good things, God would see me as a good person, and then, maybe, I would too.

As I studied the Bible, I knew what the words said, but it was impossible for me to believe the gospel message—that I was God's beloved child and He saved me because of His mercy, not because of the things I had or had not done. I kept trying to deserve His love and earn my salvation.

Thankfully, over the years, the gospel went from my head to my heart. The old scars began to heal as the good news penetrated my soul, and I began to grow in confidence and contentment—knowing without a doubt that I was, and always would be, worthy, the beloved child of God.

Think About It

Are you like I was? Do you know the good news—that you are God's beloved child—but you have problems believing it? Or maybe you aren't sure exactly what the Bible says about the good news. Either way, let's look at some passages from the Bible and see what makes us worthy to be loved by God.

According to the Bible, what makes us worthy to be loved by God?

What makes us worthy?	Scripture
Jesus' death on the cross *Holy because Jesus took on all our sin so God could look at us in our reconciled state*	Colossians 1:21–22– "Once you were alienated from God and were enemies in your minds because of your evil behavior. But now he has reconciled you by Christ's physical body through death to present you holy in his sight, without blemish and free from accusation."
Jesus' death on the cross *Christ was not a sinner therefore endured sin because of his love for us. Holy God took on our unholy sin!*	Romans 5:8– "But God demonstrates his own love for us in this: While we were still sinners, Christ died for us."
Jesus' death on the cross *If we could earn our salvation we would have no need for Christ' blood.*	Ephesians 2:8–9 (NLT)– "God saved you by his special favor when you believed. And you can't take credit for this; it is a gift from God. Salvation is not a reward for the good things we have done, so none of us can boast about it."
Jesus' death on the cross *God allowed his God-man to take on fallen humanity in order to save our souls.*	John 3:16– "For God so loved the world that he gave his one and only Son, that whoever believes in him shall not perish but have eternal life."
Jesus' death on the cross *We are forgiven over + over again because of Jesus sacrifice.*	1 Peter 2:24– "He himself bore our sins in his body on the tree, so that we might die to sins and live for righteousness." *Amen*

Works negates Christ

Write About It ✎

When you determine how worthy you are by what you do, what does that say about Jesus' death on the cross?

We are not worthy because of anything we have done, but because of Jesus' death on the cross. When we recognize that our worth comes from what Jesus did and not the things we have or have not done, we begin to feel right with God, right with the world, and right with ourselves. The Bible talks about this by calling it "righteousness."

Are you righteous?
Many Christians are confused about the term "righteousness" because they don't understand that there are two types of righteousness described in the Bible.

1. Justification–God sees us just as though we have never sinned because of our faith in Jesus.
• **Romans 5:1**— *"Therefore, since we have been justified through faith, we have peace with God through our Lord Jesus Christ."*
• The results of justification: God adopts us into His family and forgives our sins. Because of justification we can be certain that we will go to heaven.

2. Sanctification—the daily process of allowing God to help us become more like Jesus.
• **1 Thessalonians 4:3a, 7**— *"It is God's will that you should be sanctified....For God did not call us to be impure, but to live a holy life."*
• The results of sanctification: we grow in the desire and ability to do God's will. *Taking on responsibility for our sin and asking for forgiveness other · Over becoming forgiven + righteous*
Take another look at the five passages under the Think About It section. Place a "J" or "S" next to each passage, depending on the type of righteousness it describes—justification or sanctification. (Hint: one of the passages describes both.)

Answers: All five passages describe justification. The final passage, 1 Peter 2:24, describes both types of righteousness.

Here are some lies I believed about the gospel message. Do you believe any of them?
1. I must do good deeds in order to earn my salvation.
2. If my good deeds outweigh my bad ones, I'll deserve to go to heaven. *No Justified by faith.*

3. God doesn't love me when I sin. *No — Sanctified through forgiveness.*

4. I am afraid that I won't ever be good enough, so I probably won't go to heaven. *Evil lie - Justified by faith in Christ.*

5. Even though I have a loving relationship with God and have asked Jesus to be my Savior, I can't be sure I'm going to heaven when I die. *False — the lie of the enemy.*

Pray About It

Read this prayer, and if you want it to be your own prayer, sign and date it below:

God, thank You for what You said in the passages that we studied today—that because of Jesus' death on the cross, You see me as worthy—holy, without blemish and free of accusation. That is unimaginable to me! This means that I no longer have to feel ashamed and inadequate. Because Jesus died for my sins, I am pure in Your eyes. Thank You that I can't earn Your love or my salvation, but You give them to me freely because Jesus is my Savior and Lord. And thank You, God, that I am Your beloved child, called by Your name. I am a Christian, and because of Jesus' death on the cross, I can be sure that I am going to heaven when I die. Help my life to reflect the love and gratitude I feel for You.

Signed *Valerie*   **Date** 4-15-13

As you think about Today's Verse, praise God for your justification. Ask Him to help you to grow toward sanctification. Name specific areas where you need to grow. Titus 3:5 (NLT)— *"He saved us, not because of the good things we did, but because of His mercy."*

Do It

Remember: God loves you just the way you are, but He loves you too much to leave you the way you are.

Day 2
Relying on God's Help

Today's Verse

Romans 7:19 *(NLT)— "When I want to do good, I don't. And when I try not to do wrong, I do it anyway."*

Read About It

After years of dieting, starving, and bingeing, I was fatter than ever. The harder I tried not to overeat, the more I found myself eating. I had dieted a thousand times before; however, this time nothing seemed to work. My blood pressure zoomed out of control, but everything I learned in nursing school and all my willpower didn't help me to quit overeating.

Every morning I pleaded with God to help me to eat right that day. By lunchtime I found myself saying, "With all the stress at work, I just need something to get me through the day," and I gobbled up everything in sight. As soon as I got home, I would run to the refrigerator, muttering, "I've already blown it today, so I may as well eat." Every night I fell asleep promising to do better and beating myself up for eating in such an unhealthy way...again.

I knew that Philippians 4:13 said that I could do all things through Christ who strengthened me, but that verse just brought questions to my mind: Why wouldn't Jesus help me quit overeating? Was it because I wasn't a good Christian? Was there any hope for me?

That was 20 years ago—the year I lost my extra pounds and began finding answers to the questions I had been asking. Let's look at Today's Verse and the verses surrounding it to see where I found some answers.

Think About It

I love Paul's honesty! He was a faithful man of God, yet he admits in Today's Verse that he struggles with weaknesses, just as you and I do. He says that he wants to obey God, but he feels the tug of his old nature dragging him into sin.

Look at Romans 7:18 (NLT) where Paul says, *"I know I am rotten through and through so far as my old sinful nature is concerned. No matter which way I turn, I can't make myself do right. I want to, but I can't."*

Many of us can identify with him. We feel rotten through and through. And we can also identify with what he says in verses 21–24a: *"It seems to be a fact of life that when I want to do what is right, I inevitably do what is wrong. I love God's law with all my heart. But there is another law at work within me that is at war with my mind. This law wins the fight and makes me a slave to the sin that is still within me. Oh, what a miserable person I am!"*

Paul says what we already know: there is a battle in each of our minds. Our old nature wants us to sin, and our spiritual side wants to obey God. It is a tug-of-war between the two to see who will win. When our old nature is winning we feel like Paul did—miserable slaves to sin. But thankfully Paul gives us hope in the midst of battle when he says, *"Who will free me from this life that is dominated by sin?"*

I can hear the excitement in Paul's voice in verse 25 when he answers the question he just asked: *"Thank God! The answer is in Jesus Christ our Lord."*

Jesus is our hope. We have victory over our old nature through Him. But in order to experience this victory in our daily battles, we must quit beating ourselves up when our old nature pops its ugly head up. Everyone has an old nature—even people as spiritually mature as Paul. When our old nature is dragging us into sin we must turn to Jesus for help. And if we fail, we must confess and be forgiven. If we fall into shame every time we fail, our old nature wins. But if we cling to Jesus, He gives us victory.

We cling to Jesus by having a personal relationship with Him. We confess Him as our Savior and Lord and are mindful of the active presence of the living God in our lives as we go through each day.

Here are some practical ways to cling to Jesus:

• Spend 15 minutes or more first thing every morning praying and studying the Bible. An excellent way to get into this habit is by reading one daily section in *From Worthless to Worthy* and answering the questions.

• When you feel the tug of your old nature encouraging you to complain, gossip, or be impatient, dishonest, or unkind, turn to Jesus. Ask Him to help you to do what is right.

• When you fail, and are tempted to berate yourself, turn to Jesus instead. Confess what you have done and praise Him for forgiving you.

Write About It

Are you clinging to Jesus or are you too busy beating yourself up? Take these two little tests and see.

Test #1—Am I Clinging to Jesus?

Yes___ No___ 1. I have confessed Jesus as my Savior.

Yes___ No___ 2. If I do something wrong I sometimes worry that I am not really a Christian.

Yes___ No___ 3. I feel ashamed that I am not as good a Christian as most people.

Yes___ No___ 4. When I have sinned, I don't want to pray, study the Bible, or go to church.

Yes___ No___ 5. I am often too busy to pray.

Yes___ No___ 6. I often forget to turn to Jesus when I am tempted.

If your answer to the first question is no or if any of the answers to questions 2–6 is yes, you have some work to do to learn how to cling to Jesus. As you read this book, pay special attention to the practical suggestions, such as the three I just gave you, and start using some of them every day.

Test #2—Do I Beat Myself up?

Yes___ No___ 1. When I fail, I usually call myself names.

Yes___ No___ 2. I sometimes do things that are not good for me because I feel that I deserve to be punished.

Yes___ No___ 3. I often get disgusted with myself when I don't do what I want to do.

Yes___ No___ 4. I frequently gossip about myself, berating myself to others.

Yes___ No___ 5. I have given up on myself and feel that I will never change.

Yes___ No___ 6. While taking this test, I felt overwhelmed and hopeless because of some of my answers.

If your answer to any of the questions is yes, rejoice because you have identified a harmful habit that you can put a stop to. As you go through each day, try to become more aware of negative things you are thinking or saying about yourself. When you notice that you are berating yourself, stop and praise God for His unconditional love for you. There is hope for you. If I can stop beating myself up, you can too!

As you continue to reflect on Today's Verse, fill in these squares:

What do you want to do that you aren't doing?	What are you doing that you are trying not to do?

Pray About It 🙏

Reflect on Today's Verse as you pray, Romans 7:19 (NLT)— *"When I want to do good, I don't. And when I try not to do wrong, I do it anyway."* Tell God about any answers in the Write About It section that concern you. Thank Him for sending Jesus to help you to win the battle over your old nature.

_____

_____

_____

_____

_____

Father, I sometimes think that everyone else is better than I am. I measure how good a Christian I am by how well I perform. And I am often so focused on how well I am doing (or how terribly) that I don't focus on You at all. Please forgive me. Help me to stop beating myself up when I fail. Help me to cling to Jesus—relying on Him to help me to win the battle with my old nature.

Do It

You can't cling to Jesus when you are beating yourself up. When you fail, reach out to Him and rejoice in His unconditional love for you!

Day 3
Adopted by the Father

Today's Verse

Ephesians 1:5 *(NLT)*— *"His unchanging plan has always been to adopt us into his own family by bringing us to himself through Jesus Christ. And this gave him great pleasure."*

Read About It

Here is a story that shows us something about God's love: Mr. and Mrs. Joseph came into the juvenile detention center the same day Maryanne arrived. When she first saw them she was dirty, defiant, and hurting. Maryanne noticed the couple looking at her, and when their eyes met, they walked over to her. The Josephs weren't like the social workers or the police who had picked her up when she got caught taking that lady's purse. The police had remained cold and impersonal, even when they found out that she was only 14 and had been living on the streets after her mother overdosed on cocaine.

But Mr. and Mrs. Joseph seemed to really care about her. They said, "If you want to leave this place, come with us." And she went. They adopted her into their family, gave her their name, and treated her as if she were their own daughter. They bought her new clothes. She liked living with them and the other children they adopted. They gave her lots of hugs and encouragement. Mr. Joseph offered to help her with her homework any time she asked him to, but if she didn't want his help, he let her do things on her own. He told her the house rules and said that they would protect her from making mistakes.

Sometimes she broke the rules. One time she ran away, but when she returned they accepted her back with open arms, promising to love her no matter what she did. They said they loved her because she was their child, not because she was perfect. Sometimes they disciplined her, but she knew they did it out of love. Often her adoptive parents told Maryanne that they could see great potential in her.

When she saw herself through their eyes she began to believe that she was somebody worthwhile. Maryanne said, "Their love makes me want to be more like them and to bring honor to the name they gave me. It is changing my life."

Think About It

Do you see the parallels between our lives with our heavenly Father and Maryanne's life with her adopted parents?

- Undeserved mercy
- Unconditional love
- Protective rules
- Loving discipline
- Blossoming potential
- Life-changing devotion

None of us deserves God's love, but when we accept Jesus as our Savior, God adopts us into His family. We can choose to live in a loving relationship with our heavenly Father or respond in ways that are not pleasing to Him. Here are some ways we might respond to God's love:

- **Rebellion**—ignoring God and disobeying His will.
- **Entitlement**—demanding what we want and getting angry if we don't get it.
- **Complacency**—reasoning that since God loves us no matter what, we don't have to work at becoming like He wants us to be.
- **Shame**—refusing to accept God's love because we feel unworthy.
- **Gratitude**—feeling so appreciative that the God of the universe loves us that we respond as any loving child would—thanking Him for all He has done for us, spending time with Him, relying on His help, telling others about Him, obeying Him, and apologizing when we fail.

Write About It

A. Rebellion
B. Entitlement
C. Complacency
D. Shame
E. Gratitude

Place A–E from the topics above next to the following examples of things people say in response to God's love:

___ 1. If I don't get my way, I get mad at God.

___ 2. I'm too busy to obey God, even though I know what He wants me to do.

___ 3. I am such a bad person that God can't possibly love me.

___ 4. When I see the love God has for me, I want to become everything He wants me to be.

___ 5. I know God loves me and understands that I don't like to do anything that requires discipline.

Answers: 1B, 2A, 3D, 4E, 5C

Now reread the list above and place a check next to ways you respond to God's love.

Take a Look at Your Parents
Some of us didn't have parents who modeled God's love to us. Those of us who were rejected or harshly criticized by our parents tend to believe that God feels the same way about us, but that is far from the truth. Look at the following verses that describe the qualities of God. Thankfully, He doesn't have the same limitations as some of our parents. Place a check next to any negative traits that your parents had.

Bible verses that tell us what God is like:

God is merciful and forgiving, but some of our parents were angry, unforgiving, or even violent. Daniel 9:9— *"The Lord our God is merciful and forgiving, even though we have rebelled against him."*

God is powerful, mighty, and strong, while some of our parents were weak. Isaiah 40:26— *"Lift your eyes and look to the heavens: Who created all these? He who brings out the starry host one by one, and calls them each by name. Because* *of his great power and mighty strength, not one of them is missing."*

God is intimate, available, and close, while some of our parents were distant. Isaiah 41:13— *"For I am the LORD, your God, who takes hold of your right hand and says to you, Do not fear; I will help you."*

God is generous and sacrificing, while some of our parents were selfish and self-serving. Romans 8:32— *"He who did not spare his own Son, but gave him up for us all— how will he not also, along with him, graciously give us all things?"*

God is trustworthy and dependable, while some of our parents were inconsistent and unreliable. 1 Samuel 15:29— *"He who is the Glory of Israel does not lie or change his mind; for he is not a man, that he should change his mind."*

God is compassionate and gracious, while some of our parents were unloving. Psalm 103:8— *"The LORD is compassionate and gracious, slow to anger, abounding in love."*

God is faithful, while some of our parents were rejecting. Romans 8:39— *"Neither height nor depth, nor anything else in all creation, will be able to separate us from the love of God that is in Christ Jesus our Lord."*

God is involved in our lives, while some of our parents seemed to be uncaring. Matthew 10:30— *"And even the very hairs of your head are all numbered."*

God is wise, while many of our parents were very unwise. Daniel 2:21— *"He gives wisdom to the wise and knowledge to the discerning."*

Write about the effect your parents' negative qualities have had on your life. Look at it realistically, but don't make the mistake of falling into self-pity.

_____

_____

_____

_____

_____

_____

Pray About It 🙏

Look at the quality of God and the verse above that corresponds to each negative quality you checked about your parents. Pray, praising God for His qualities.

As you read the following prayer, reflect on Today's Verse. Ephesians 1:5 (NLT)— *"His unchanging plan has always been to adopt us into his own family by bringing us to himself through Jesus Christ. And this gave him great pleasure."*

God, I thank You for adopting me into Your family. It amazes me when I think that the God of the universe chose me to be His beloved child. You love me far more than any earthly parent could. You want to have a close relationship with me. You want me to spend time with You and rely on You for direction and help. It grieves You when I sin. Thank You that You are not a harsh judge, ready to punish me the minute I make a mistake. Instead, You are my precious Father who loves me perfectly, completely, and unconditionally.

Do It 👣

Saint Augustine said, "Love slays what we have been, that we may be what we were not." Bask in the light of God's love today!

Day 4
Chosen for a Purpose

Today's Verse

1 Corinthians 1:27 (NLT)— *"God deliberately chose things the world considers foolish in order to shame those who think they are wise. And he chose those who are powerless to shame those who are powerful."*

Read About It

Even when I was a little girl I wanted to make a difference in the world. I really wanted to help people, but how could I? I couldn't even help myself. I was insecure, overweight, unhappy, and a worrywart. I didn't understand the exciting truth in Today's Verse then, but I do now. I have learned that when we surrender our lives to the Lord, God takes our mistakes, our weaknesses, our hurts, and even our past sins and uses them for our good and His glory. And He chooses us for specific work in His kingdom because of our unique qualifications.

The world may consider us foolish, but God doesn't. When we cooperate with Him, He uses us to do things that "wise" people could never do. God is using me to help others, not in spite of my weaknesses, but because of them.

It is amazing that this formerly insecure ex-worrywart loves going on TV and speaking before large audiences. Most of the time I do so with confidence and delight because I love to tell the story of how God is changing me. How exciting it is to see God using my struggles to help others know Him and experience His wisdom and power.

Think About It

Think about the people in the Bible whom God used most. Here are a few examples:

• **Moses**—a baby left on a doorstep (actually, in a river) who later murdered someone and went into hiding for 40 years.

• **David**—a shepherd who later committed adultery and murder.

• **Mary Magdalene**—a woman who had seven evil spirits which Jesus cast out.

• **Peter, Andrew, James and John**—common fishermen, who seldom understood, bickered jealously, and fell asleep when they were needed most.

God uses people who have made mistakes and have weaknesses—people the world considers foolish and powerless... like you and me. Why do you think He does that? Let's look at three verses to find some possible reasons.

____ **1. Acts 4:13**— *"When they saw the courage of Peter and John and realized that they were unschooled, ordinary men, they were astonished and they took note that these men had been with Jesus."*

____ **2. Matthew 9:13b**— [Jesus said] *"I have not come to call the righteous, but sinners."*

____ **3. 2 Corinthians 1:4** (NLT)— *"When others are troubled, we will be able to give them the same comfort God has given us."*

Below are some reasons why God may use people the world considers foolish and powerless. **Place the letter with each of the following reasons next to the appropriate verse above.**

A. When God has helped us overcome a problem, we can help others in a similar situation if we are willing to share openly with them.
B. When we surrender our lives to the Lord and He begins to change us, people take note and know that we have been with Jesus.
C. When we recognize our sinfulness and realize how much we need Jesus, we become desperate for His help and allow Him to work in us.

Answers: 1B, 2C, 3A

Write About It

Today you are going to write your resume. Instead of including all of the things that you are proud of, this resume will include the things that make you feel most ashamed. List below your biggest hurt, weakness, and mistake.

My Resume

My biggest hurt:

My biggest weakness:

My biggest mistake:

Now I want you to look on these things in a different light. Look at them as opportunities for Christ to work in you, to display His power in you, and use you to help others. As God helps you to overcome these things, your faith will grow and it will be contagious. You will be able to help countless others by telling them about what God is doing in your life. Nothing is too terrible to be used by God. No one is out of His reach, no matter how far they have strayed from Him and His ways.

Turn your misery into ministry!

Let me give you some examples of women who have allowed God to use their problems, and other women who have stayed stuck in them:

• I know two women. Both are Christians. Both are going through financial ruin and bankruptcy. One is having a nervous breakdown, and the other is busy praising God for His sufficiency to supply all her needs even though she has almost nothing.

• I know two other women. Both are Christians. Both found out that their husbands have been unfaithful. One is depressed and bitter, even though her husband is repentant and wants to reconcile. The other rejoices in God's sufficiency, even though she has four young children and her husband married the other woman.

• I know two other women who have lost children. One lost her fifth child at birth ten years ago and, according to her, has never been happy since. The other lost her ten-year-old daughter to leukemia and praises the Lord for comforting her and providing her with a new ministry helping other parents who have lost children.

What is the difference between the two women in each example?

_____

_____

_____

There are several right answers to that question, but I believe the answer that sums them all up is this: **Some of these women are putting their hope in God and some are not. They are stuck in self-pity, depression, resentment, or shame.** It is important to remember that none of us trusts God perfectly. When we are going through trials, all of us have to deal with negative feelings so we don't get stuck in them.

In the examples, if you identify more with the women who are stuck, I know how you feel. I spent many years stuck. I knew that God wanted to help me, but I didn't know how to let Him. During the past 30 years I have been learning new ways to put my hope in God and let Him work in my life. *From Worthless to Worthy* is full of these ways. If you feel stuck, determine to continue working through this book and applying the lessons inside. You also might consider starting a small group by using the Leader's Guide in the back of this book and sharing the things you are learning with others.

Pray About It

Reflect on Today's Verse as you ask God to show you ways to help others by using something on your "resume." 1 Corinthians 1:27 (NLT)— *"God deliberately chose things the world considers foolish in order to shame those who think they are wise. And he chose those who are powerless to shame those who are powerful."*

Lord, help me to put my hope in You—to be confident that You have chosen me and will use me to help others. Help me to depend on You and make You my firm foundation so I won't stay stuck in my problems. I admit that I have done many foolish things and that, without Your help, I am power-less to change. Thank You that with this admission comes true hope because I am no longer putting my hope in myself or in others, but in You. Help me to draw closer to You every day and trust You to change me and use me according to Your will.

Do It

Remember that God even used a donkey to speak for Him (Numbers 22:28), so He can certainly use us!

Day 5
Rejoicing in God's Faithfulness

Today's Verse

Isaiah 49:15–16a— *"Can a mother forget the baby at her breast and have no compassion on the child she has borne? Though she may forget, I will not forget you! See, I have engraved you on the palms of my hands."*

Read About It

Joe had known since high school that he couldn't handle alcohol. The first time he and his buddies went out to drink he drank too much. But it felt so good. Drinking helped knock down the walls he built up around himself, and it helped numb the pain of never fitting in or feeling good about who he was.

Soon his drinking became more and more uncontrollable. One night, when caught staggering into the house, the words his father spewed at Joe became a prophecy that would haunt him: "You're going to end up a drunk like me."

After four years of binges and broken promises, the incredible happened. Joe quit drinking. It happened suddenly, miraculously. One of Joe's friends insisted that he go to church with him, and in that small country church Joe met Jesus. The pastor told Joe that his drinking problems were covered by the blood of Christ, and Joe was set free. His life changed instantly and Joe not only stopped drinking, but he started studying the Bible and telling everyone about his miracle.

After a year or so, Joe got a job and moved to a new city. Some of his new friends invited him to go out for a drink.

Joe planned to have a Coke, but for some reason he didn't. His friends drove him home that night to sleep it off. After that, Joe's drinking was more out of control than ever. He kept calling out to God, but Joe couldn't stop drinking.

One morning as Joe brushed his teeth, trying to get the hangover taste out of his mouth, he was shocked to see a disheveled drunk looking back at him in the mirror. Immediately his father's prophecy echoed in his throbbing head: "You're going to end up a drunk like me." Joe fell on his bed sobbing and begged God to heal him like He had before. As Joe prayed, he felt compelled to call a church. He found one in the phone book. Within 30 minutes of making the call, Joe was sitting in the pastor's office tearfully asking: *"Is there any hope for me? Has God given up on me?"*

Think About It

Today's Verse draws two beautiful word pictures to reassure us that God never gives up on us. Look at the first word picture above. What can be more personal than a mother breast-feeding a baby? She is giving of herself to provide for the needs of her infant. She isn't concerned about whether the baby deserves to be fed. She doesn't say, "My baby cried too much yesterday, so I won't feed him today." God assures us that He is like a compassionate mother who loves her baby.

In the second word picture God says, "See, I have engraved you on the palms of my hands..." Before we were married, my husband and I were out walking one beautiful spring day when he stopped, took out his pocket knife, and engraved my name on a tree. I really appreciated that romantic deed. But even though it was romantic, it wasn't sacrificial. It didn't cost him anything or hurt him in any way. God tells us that His love is sacrificial. He experienced pain to prove His love for us. Engraving our names on the palms of His hands—and sending His Son to die for us—weren't things He took lightly, and they weren't things He would take back.

God is speaking through these two word pictures to Joe and the rest of us. He is saying this:

> You are My beloved child. I am devoted to you. My love is personal, sacrificial, and permanent. I am fully committed to you forever.

• **Does God remain committed to us even when we sin?** Yes, even when we sin. 1 John 2:1— *"My dear children, I write this to you so that you will not sin. But if anybody does sin, we have one who speaks to the Father in our defense— Jesus Christ, the Righteous One."*

• **Does God remain committed to us even when we sin again and again?** Yes, even when we sin again and again. 1 John 1:9— *"If we confess our sins, he is faithful and just and will forgive us our sins and purify us from all unrighteousness."*

• **Since God forgives us when we sin, does it mean that our sins don't matter?** To find an answer, let's look at Psalm 103:13— *"As a father has compassion on his children, so the LORD has compassion on those who fear him."* This verse says that God has compassion on His children when they fear Him. What does that mean?

Fear means "to be in awe of, to respect, to revere." When you disobey your heavenly Father you are obviously not showing awe or respect for Him. If you disregard His will, He will find it necessary, like any good parent, to discipline you. Proverbs 3:12a explains this: *"The LORD disciplines those he loves."*

Write About It ✏

We will summarize each of the main points made today by looking again at the three word pictures that describe each point. Answer the following questions after you have filled in the blanks:

1. We are God's beloved children. Isaiah 49:15— *"Can a _____ forget the _____?"*

Yes___ No___ **Is the thought that God loves you so tenderly going from your head to your heart?**

If you are still struggling with this, pray for God to help you to understand this amazing promise. If you have confessed Jesus as your Savior and desire to believe the truth from His Word, God will help you to know in your heart that you are His child.

2. God is devoted to us—personally, sacrificially and permanently. Isaiah 49:16 *"See I have _____ you on _____."*

Yes___ No___ **Do you believe that God is devoted to you in this way?**

If your answer was *no*, pray for God to help you to understand His love. Consider going to your pastor or a respected Christian friend and talking to him or her about it.

3. Sometimes God responds with compassion, and sometimes with discipline. Psalm 103:13— *"As a _____ has compassion on his _____ so the Lord has compassion on those who _____ him."*

List ways you are not showing fear of the Lord:

_____

_____

_____

_____

Not all trials are due to God's discipline, but some are. List ways God may be disciplining you:

_____

_____

_____

Pray About It 🙏

Reflect on Today's Verse as you pray, thanking God for being a loving Father who will never give up on you. Isaiah 49:16a— *"See, I have engraved you on the palms of my hands."*

Lord, thank You for choosing me to be Your child and for being so committed to me. And thank You for drawing these beautiful word pictures to help me understand how tenderly You love me. Help me to believe the truth from Your Word about myself rather than believing my negative feelings or the condemning words of others. Help me to finally understand that I am Yours and You love me with all Your heart. And, Father, give me the willingness and ability to draw closer to You, trust You, and obey You.

Do It 👣

God is devoted to you—personally, sacrificially, and permanently. Look back on how you spent your thoughts, words, and actions during the last 24 hours. What are you devoted to?

Chapter 2

How Can I Experience God's Power at Work in Me?

Day 6

Confessing My Sins

Today's Verse

Psalm 51:2 *(NLT)— "Wash me clean from my guilt. Purify me from my sin."*

Read About It

Janet knocked hesitantly on the door of my church's counseling office, where she had come to talk to me. A 35-year-old working mother, whose attractiveness was only slightly marred by her wrinkled brow and down-turned lips, Janet seemed to have what others envy—good looks, a nice husband, two children, and enough money to get by on. But Janet was miserable, and when I asked her what she wanted to talk about, she blurted out what had been bothering her for a long time.

"I feel so guilty all the time. I scream at my kids and my husband. I try not to, but I can't help it. And to make matters worse, I used to be close to the Lord, but I have drifted away from Him. I pray sometimes in the car, but I never go to church or read the Bible anymore. I just don't have time, and whenever I think about it, I feel like a hypocrite because I know my life isn't pleasing to the Lord. I want His help, but don't know how to get it. Is there any hope for me?"

Janet's problem is shared by millions of Christians across the country. We are all so busy, and even though we know that Jesus died to free us from our sins, we remain weighed down by guilt. Rather than drawing us back to God, our guilt builds walls between us and God. We feel hopeless and overwhelmed—desperately wanting God's help, but not knowing how to get it.

Working with Janet for the next several weeks was a privilege. After she confessed her sins and became willing to make a few changes, it was exciting to see God at work in her life. Janet learned how to accept His forgiveness and begin the process of relying on His power one day at a time.

Think About It

As you read Janet's statements, did you identify with her? Place a check next to any of these questions that you might answer with a *yes*.

• Do you feel guilty over something?
• Do you feel that you are drifting away from the Lord?
• Do you want God's help, but don't know how to get it?

Unconfessed sin is the primary thing that blocks God's power at work in Christians. So the first thing we will focus on is how to confess our sins. David's prayer in Psalm 51 gives us a wonderful model of confession, so let's get to work and study David's confession.

Many believe that David wrote this psalm when confronted by Nathan the prophet after David had done something unthinkable: this man of God committed adultery with Bathsheba and then had her husband killed! But because David confessed his sins to God, God forgave him and we have this model of confession to use today.

David's Model Confession from Psalm 51 (NLT)

1. Psalm 51:1a— *"Have mercy on me, O God, because of your unfailing love."* David reminds himself of God's love as he throws himself on His mercy. He pleads guilty before the Lord—with no excuses or self-justification.

2. Psalm 51:2— *"Wash me clean from my guilt. Purify me from my sin."* David knows that God can completely remove all of his sins as well as the guilt he feels.

3. Psalm 51:12— *"Restore to me again the joy of your salvation, and make me willing to obey you."* David thinks about the joy that he had when he was close to God, and prays for willingness to obey Him. David knows if he continues in disobedience, he will not experience true joy.

4. Psalm 51:13— *"Then I will teach your ways to sinners, and they will return to you."* David thinks about how God can use his experience to help others.

5. Psalm 51:16a— *"You would not be pleased with sacrifices, or I would bring them."* David realizes that he can't pay for his sins by punishing himself or doing good deeds for others.

6. Psalm 51:17a— *"The sacrifice you want is a broken spirit."* David realizes that God wants him to quit acting like a high-spirited horse—bucking when called to serve others, refusing to learn, and running away from his master. Instead, God wants him to be humble, teachable, and repentant.

Write About It ✏

How do you confess your sins? Let's use David's model from Psalm 51 and confess our sins to the Lord. Use your prayer journal to write on the suggested topics.

1. Throw yourself on God's mercy. Pour out your heart to God in your prayer journal. Tell Him every unconfessed sin that comes to your mind. If you have confessed a sin but you continue to repeat it, confess it again! Don't give any excuses or try to justify yourself in any way.

2. Know that no matter what you have done, God will cleanse you because of your faith in Jesus. Memorize 1 John 1:9— *"If we confess our sins, he is faithful and just and will forgive us our sins and purify us from all unrighteousness."*

3. Pray for willingness to obey God. Are you committing any sins you are not ready to give up? If so, list them in your prayer journal and pray for willingness to obey God. Write about what these sins are costing you.

4. Think about how God can use your experience to help others. Write a prayer asking God to use your experience to help others.

5. Don't try to pay for your sins by doing good deeds or by punishing yourself. If you have been, write about this and praise God that your sins were paid for at the cross.

6. Come to God with a broken spirit. Don't be like a high-spirited horse—instead, be humble, teachable, and repentant.

Compare the way that you confessed with the way that a "modern sinner" may confess. Read this to see how *not* to confess your sins. Underline anything in the "prayer" that reminds you of confessions you have made.

Misinterpretation of Psalm 51

"Forgive me, God, because I was reared in a dysfunctional family and I can't help myself. You created me the way I am, and I am only human, so I can't change. God, make me feel good about myself. I know that all I have to do is say, "I'm sorry," and anything I continue to do is okay. Create in me a happy heart, O God. I deserve it because basically I am a good person. Don't take my good life away from me. Restore to me the happiness that I had before and grant me my desires. I know that You appreciate the sacrifice I make two Sundays a month when I go to church and the money that I have given to the poor."

Pray About It 🙏

Pray as you consider Today's Verse, Psalm 51:2 (NLT)— *"Wash me clean from my guilt. Purify me from my sin."*

Father, thank You so much that You have mercy on me when I confess my sins to You because You know that I am truly sorry. Thank You for sending Jesus to pay the price for my sins so that, no matter what I have done, when I confess to You, I literally come clean—You see me just as though I never sinned. Lord, please restore to me the joy I had when I was walking closer to You. Help me to obey You in everything I think, say, and do. Help me not to cover up my sins, but to help others not to make the same mistakes. I know that I can't pay the price for my sins by feeling bad about myself or doing good deeds. What You want is for me to humbly confess my sins to You, rejoicing that You will remove my guilt, replace it with joy, and help me to obey You.

Do It 👣

Come clean and confess your sins to the Lord and you will literally come clean! He will see you just as though you had never sinned.

Day 7
Humbling (NOT Humiliating) Myself

Today's Verse

1 Peter 5:6— *"Humble yourselves, therefore, under God's mighty hand, that he may lift you up in due time."*

Read About It

I ran into an old friend at a writers' conference a few months ago. Mary had just finished writing her first book. It was a how-to book about raising Christian teenagers. As she spoke, her frustration started pouring out. She sighed deeply as she said, "I have worked so hard trying to get this book published, but everyone I submitted it to rejected it. I feel like I have really let God down." Then she smiled and added, "At least there's one bright spot in all of this. I know that God hates pride, and humility comes naturally to me right now because I feel so bad about myself!"

Mary thought she was being humble, but she wasn't humble at all. She was humiliated.

Think About It

Humiliation is a feeling of disgrace.

• It is the result of looking at your weaknesses without remembering that God is there to give you His strength.

• It is looking at your failures without remembering that God will use them to help you learn.

• It is looking at your sins without remembering that God sent Jesus to pay the price for them on the cross.

• Humiliation has something in common with pride: they

both focus on self, independent of God. Out of seeds of humiliation grows a deep sense of shame and hopelessness.

> People who are humiliated look at themselves apart from God, while humble people look at themselves embraced by God.

Although humiliation and humility are opposites, many Christians, like Mary, believe that they are the same thing.

Humility comes when we have a deep understanding of Today's Verse. It comes when...

• We recognize *God's mighty hand* and know that everything that happens to us must pass through His fingers first.

• We recognize that God knows best, and we put our hope in Him, trusting that *He will lift us up in due time.* We desire His will above our own and quit wandering off without Him into worry, self-sufficiency, or disobedience.

• We recognize our weakness in light of God's strength. We determine to stay close to Him and rely on His mighty power instead of our flimsy self-efforts.

> Humility comes when we can say this prayer and mean it: "Everything I need comes from You, O Lord. I am open to receive it. I face this day and all of life knowing that You will supply all of my needs."

When we disobey, we must draw close to the Lord, humbly confess our sins, and ask for His help. We must keep our focus on Him and rely on His grace to give us the desire and ability to do His will. And just as important, we must also rely on His forgiveness when we fail.

Let's look at Mary again so that we can learn from her mistakes.

• If Mary were humble, she wouldn't worry about "letting God down." Mary would realize that she can't lift God up or let Him down. Those words draw a vivid picture that shows Mary's lack of humility.

• If Mary were humble, she would put her dream of getting her book published in God's hands. She would be aware of her job—to pray, draw close to God, write, and submit what she has written. And Mary would be aware of God's job—to inspire her writing and open the publishing house doors at the right time.

• If Mary were humble, she wouldn't feel terrible about herself when her work didn't turn out as she had planned. She would keep writing and submitting her work as long as that desire was in her heart. She would feel good about herself during this process because she would know that God loves her and has plans to use her to help others…in due time.

• If Mary were humble, she would know that her responsibility is to respond to God's ability.

Write About It ✐

Take this little quiz to see if you are humble or humiliated. Think carefully before answering so you won't check the "right" answer, but the answer that is true for you.

Are You Humble or Humiliated?

1. When someone criticizes me…
   A. I get defensive and point out the person's faults.
   B. I thank the person for telling me and later pray about whether the criticism was valid.
2. When I have a problem…
   A. I stay busy so I don't have to deal with it.
   B. I turn to God and ask for His help.
3. When I make a mistake…
   A. I cover it up the best I can and hope no one notices.
   B. I admit it to myself and others who are directly involved.

4. When someone gives me a compliment...
   A. I feel good about myself, but pretend that I don't deserve praise.
   B. I thank the person for the compliment, and God for His power.
5. When an acquaintance admits a weakness and I struggle with it too...
   A. I don't mention that I have the same problem, so she won't judge me.
   B. I tell her about my problem.
6. When I recognize a weakness...
   A. I feel ashamed of myself.
   B. I draw closer to God and know that He will use my weakness for good if I rely on His strength.
7. When I have had an argument with my husband on Sunday morning...
   A. I don't go to church because I feel too bad about myself.
   B. I go to church to receive encouragement as I pray and worship.
8. When I have to do something that I don't feel qualified to do...
   A. I worry about it and put off doing it.
   B. I pray about it, trust God to help me, and try it.
9. When I realize that I can't do something perfectly...
   A. I give up and do it terribly, or not at all.
   B. I do the best I can while praying for God's help.
10. When I sin in a terrible way...
   A. I spend several days feeling ashamed and overwhelmed.
   B. I go to God and confess it to Him almost immediately.

Now look at your quiz and see how many A answers you have—symptoms of humiliation, and B answers—symptoms of humility.

Pray About It 🙏

Reflect on Today's Verse and quiz as you ask God to help you to be humble. 1 Peter 5:6— *"Humble yourselves, therefore, under God's mighty hand, that he may lift you up in due time."*

Lord, thank You for this command to be humble and the promise that goes with it. If I humble myself under Your mighty hand, You will lift me up in due time. When I stop to think about this verse, I see the word picture that You are drawing for me in it: Your mighty hand is there providing everything I need and reaching out to help me. If I reject Your hand because of my pride or humiliation, You will not lift me up. Instead, You will allow me to remain in my lowly state. It is only when I realize how much I need You and humbly take Your hand that You will lift me up and help me to feel good about myself. Help me today to humble myself and take the hand that You are holding out to me.

Do It 👣

Remember this as you face each problem: My responsibility is to respond to God's ability.

Day 8
Appropriating God's Grace

Today's Verse

Hebrews 4:16— *"Let us then approach the throne of grace with confidence, so that we may receive mercy and find grace to help us in our time of need."*

Read About It

"I don't need a crutch like God to lean on!" That was the proud pronouncement of agnosticism I made when I was in college. Agnostics were smart, confident, and smug. They could handle things on their own, or so I thought.

Ten years later I was falling on my face. I had everything I wanted—a wonderful husband, a baby, a good job, a new house. But I also had a truckload of resentments, paralyzing inferiority, guilt that never quit, and sky-high blood pressure.

Finally, because I was afraid I would have a stroke, I admitted what everyone else knew: I wasn't handling things very well. My doctor invited me to a Christian support group he was leading. I didn't tell him I was agnostic. The night of the first meeting I was nervous, but everyone there was friendly. After Dr. Jones introduced everyone, he got down to work.

"What bothers you most," he asked, "fear, inferiority, or guilt?" I was the first one Dr. Jones asked. The answer that sprang from my mouth astonished me. "All three of them bother me," I cried. "I feel inferior in every way. I am a terrible teacher, a terrible mother, and a terrible wife. I feel guilty for everything I do. And I am afraid there is no hope for me and I'll never change."

During the next several months my doctor and my little group helped me to understand God's grace. They shared this life-changing promise with me: **If you confess Jesus as your Savior, you can come to God with all your problems, and by His grace, He will help you in unimaginable ways!** That was more than 30 years ago, and I am truly amazed at how God has kept that promise.

Think About It

> Because of our faith in Jesus, God lavishes us with grace. Grace is God's unmerited favor of us and unlimited power in us.

Read these verses, keeping that definition of grace in mind.

___ A. Ephesians 2:8–9— *"For it is by grace you have been saved, through faith—and this not from yourselves, it is the gift of God—not by works, so that no one can boast."*

___ B. Romans 3:23–24a— *"All have sinned and fall short of the glory of God, and are justified freely by his grace."*

___ C. 2 Corinthians 12:9a— *"But he [God] said to me, 'My grace is sufficient for you, for my power is made perfect in weakness.'"*

___ D. James 4:6b— *"God opposes the proud but gives grace to the humble."*

___ E. Galatians 2:21— *"I do not set aside the grace of God, for if righteousness could be gained through the law, Christ died for nothing!"*

___ F. 2 Peter 3:18a— *"But grow in the grace and knowledge of our Lord and Savior Jesus Christ."*

___ G. 2 Corinthians 9:8— *"And God is able to make all grace abound to you, so that in all things at all times, having all that you need, you will abound in every good work."*

Place numbers 1–7, from the statements below, next to the corresponding passage about grace above.

1. When we depend on our own righteousness we are wasting the cross.
2. God commands us to grow in grace.
3. Grace is a gift that God gives to each of us when we confess Jesus as our Savior.
4. We can't be good enough to deserve God's grace.
5. Through grace we can do every good work that God wants us to do.
6. God changes our weaknesses to strengths by His grace.
7. If we refuse to come to God for help, we won't experience His grace.

Answers: 3A, 4B, 6C, 7D, 1E, 2F, 5G

Write About It ✎

Grace is a gift that God gives to each of us when we accept Jesus as our Savior. But in order to experience the full benefit of this gift we have a responsibility. Let me explain: Let's say it's my birthday and you bring me a gift. Is it useful to me the minute you walk in the door? No. I must do several things before it is useful to me:

1. I must know that the gift is for me.
2. I must accept the gift gladly.
3. I must open it up and see what it is.
4. I must use it.

In church terminology: I must "appropriate God's grace." It is not until I know it is mine and try it out that I can benefit fully from it.

You don't have to be agnostic like I was to refuse the gift of God's grace. Lots of Christians act like agnostics—they face their problems, their decisions, their failures, and their fears as if they aren't sure that God is there or that Jesus died for their sins. There are many things we can do to appropriate God's grace. Before we talk about these things, think about this statement:

> You can't work to earn God's grace, but you have to work at appropriating it.

That statement is a paradox. At first glance it seems contradictory, but it's not. There is no way that by doing good works we can earn God's grace—making us worthy to deserve His favor. But there are many things that we must do in order to accept the gift of grace that God is offering us. Here are some of them. Check the ones that you want to start doing.

☐ Come to God with your problems every day and ask for His help.

☐ Memorize promises about God's grace and bring them to mind when you need encouragement. (2 Corinthians 12:9 and 2 Corinthians 9:8 are my favorites.)

☐ Pray for God to help you when you are tempted to do something wrong.

☐ Praise God for His grace after you confess a sin instead of beating yourself up.

☐ Record times that God has shown you His grace by answering a prayer.

☐ Tell others about how God is helping you.

☐ Reject thoughts that tell you you have to work hard to earn God's grace.

☐ Quit pretending you don't need God's grace.

☐ Step out of your comfort zone and do what God is leading you to do by relying on Him.

Look again at the above passages about grace and answer the following questions.

Yes___ No___ Are you trying to do good works to earn your salvation?

Yes___ No___ Do you feel that you are too sinful to be justified by God's grace (seen by God just as though you have never sinned)?

Yes___ No___ Do you fall for the lie that your weaknesses make it harder for you to experience God's grace?

Yes___ No___ Do you try to pretend to God and others that you have it all together?

Yes___ No___ Do you frequently berate yourself when you sin rather than praising God for forgiving you through His grace?

What are you doing to grow in grace? _____

_____

What good works require God's grace for you to do?

_____

_____

Pray About It

As you pray, reflect on Today's Verse and any answers to the quiz that concern you, thanking God for His grace. Hebrews 4:16— *"Let us then approach the throne of grace with confidence, so that we may receive mercy and find grace to help us in our time of need."*

God, thank You that I can approach Your throne with confidence, not in who I am, but in Whose I am. Because of what Jesus did for me on the cross, I am Your beloved child. I can come to You any time to ask for help with any problem I face, no matter how small. And because of Your grace I can be sure that You forgive any sin that I confess to You, no matter how big it is, how many sins I have, or how many times I have come confessing the same sin to You. Help me to step out in faith and do what You are leading me to do, because I am sure that, through Your grace, I will have the desire and ability to do Your will.

Do It

Grace is free, but not cheap. Don't waste it! It cost the life of God's Son.

Day 9
Being Changed by God's Word

Today's Verse

Hebrews 4:12— *"For the word of God is living and active. Sharper than any double-edged sword."*

Read About It

Louis was my frightened patient. He was dying of cancer inch by inch. Every morning I had to do a 45-minute treatment on him, which required both of my hands. I can still see the desperate look on Louis' face as he pleaded, "Tell me a verse from the Bible so I won't be so scared." I hate to admit it, but even though I had been a Christian for almost 10 years, I had not memorized anything except John 3:16 and part of the 23rd Psalm. After I fumbled my way through these few verses, I went home and started spending a few minutes every day memorizing Scripture so I would be better prepared to apply this healing salve to my patients' wounds. But I didn't realize that doing this would also provide healing for a lot of my wounds as well.

I'm amazed to see how memorizing Scripture has changed my life. Because I consistently memorize Scripture, God's promises are there inside of me to encourage me and help me to trust Him. His commands spring into my mind to keep me from getting off track. When I hear something contrary to Scripture, I know it and can often point to specific verses that refute it. When I am praying, I am able to pray back Scripture word by word. I believe that this is the most effective type of praying, because I am using God's very own words. At night when I can't sleep, I don't count sheep; I recall Scriptures that help me to relax. There's no better way to absorb God's

Word into our minds and hearts than to memorize it. That's why memorizing is called "learning by heart"!

Think About It

Today's Verse says God's Word is living and active, sharper than any double-edged sword. It penetrates to the deepest part of us and dissects our innermost thoughts and attitudes. His Word cuts through our defense mechanisms and excuses. It gets to the root of our problems. God's Word is a razor-sharp scalpel that can remove malignant thoughts. These thoughts can kill our spirits, contaminate our attitudes, and spread to every part of our being. But when we submit ourselves to His Word, God uses His Word to heal our hurts.

The best way to memorize Scripture is to spend just three minutes a day doing it. I started out by trying to memorize a few short passages every week, but I got frustrated because I kept forgetting the verses I had already learned. I didn't understand two important things: everyone loses what they memorize unless they have a photographic memory, and those things aren't lost permanently—they're just temporarily covered up.

When we memorize, pathways are established in our brains that can actually be visualized with special microscopes. After a few minutes other things fall on the path that was established. Soon the clutter obliterates the path, but the path is still there. We just need to brush it off a little. When I forget what I memorized the day before, I can rest assured that the pathway is still there, so I get to work brushing it off as I brush up on the passage.

Memorizing Tips
• Write the passage on the right side of a sheet of paper, folded in half (the long way). Write it neatly, in big letters, one phrase per line. If there is a list in the passage, number the items. If there are contrasting things mentioned, place them next to each other so you can easily compare them.

Note repeated words or words that start with the same letter. On the left side of the paper, write the reference and hints, such as the first letter in each phrase or little cartoons that will prod your memory. The more ridiculous the cartoons, the more likely you will remember them.

• Try to write the passage on another sheet of paper while looking only at the left side where you wrote the reference, hints, and cartoons.

• Correct what you wrote with ink that is a different color to make what you need to learn stand out.

• Eventually, write the passage without looking at anything except a blank sheet of paper.

• Put the passage on a 3 x 5 card for your purse, your bathroom, your car, your telephone, or beside your sink. That way, it will be handy so you can memorize any time.

At times, I enjoy this so much that I spend more than three minutes learning the verses. Sometimes I use my memorizing time just to review verses that I have already learned. I am no longer surprised or even frustrated when I can't remember some of them because I know that, when I review, I can learn them again in no time.

How do you choose a passage? Memorize any passage that touches your heart. When God brings it to your attention, write it in your prayer journal in a section just for Scripture. If you don't write it down right away, you'll soon forget it. Keep all your memory work together so you can review each passage from time to time.

Write About It ✏️

There are many blessings that come with memorizing Scripture. Reread what I said in the Read About It section and see if you can find all seven blessings I listed. List here ones that encourage you to memorize Scripture more.

_____

_____

_____

Here is another reason for memorizing Scripture on a regular basis: Recent studies show that the chance of getting senile dementia and Alzheimer's disease may be reduced when people consistently challenge their brains by doing things like memorizing.

Feed Your Soul with M&Ms!

In addition to memorizing Scripture, another wonderful way to use God's Word is to write a meditation on it. People in a class I was teaching on writing meditations and memorizing Scripture teased me about my M&Ms! They know that I don't eat the other kind, but my type of M&Ms feeds my soul and brings true satisfaction. In order to do meditations, begin by reading a short portion (maybe just a paragraph) of the Bible every morning. Read it *expectantly* for a few minutes—knowing that God will speak to you through His Word. In Isaiah 55:11, God promises that that the Word that goes out from His mouth will not return to Him empty, but will accomplish what He desires and achieve the purpose for which He sent it. After you have read the passage, do the following:

• Thank God for the Word He is giving you that day and pray for understanding.

• Choose one verse from the portion you read that day.

• Write the verse you chose on the top of a page in your prayer journal.

• Write God a short letter while reflecting on what you are going through that day, and tell Him what this passage means to you personally.

If you want examples of meditations on Scripture, read the prayers I have written in each Pray About It section. If you write meditations on Scripture, it will help you to apply God's Word to your circumstances in exciting ways. It truly will change your life.

Pray About It

Meditate on Today's Verse as you thank God for ways His Word helps you. Hebrews 4:12— *"For the word of God is living and active. Sharper than any double-edged sword."*

Lord, thank You so much for speaking to me personally through Your life-changing Word. It is like a supernatural channel between You and me. I can read it and receive instruction or encouragement from You about a problem I am facing today. I can read a psalm of David and enter into praise with him. I can read one of Your promises and find rest for my soul, and I can read one of Your commands and know immediately what You would have me do. Thank You for giving me Your Word and for making it alive and active inside of me when I read it with an expectant heart.

Do It

Feed your soul with M&Ms—meditation and memorization!

Day 10
Finding My Identity in Christ

Today's Verse

Philippians 3:7— *"But whatever was to my profit I now consider loss for the sake of Christ."*

Read About It

Susan has been married for ten years...ten very long years. When the 40-year-old homemaker and mother of two came dragging into my office, she looked like she had been beaten down for a long time. Sadness filled her eyes as she spoke, and she suddenly looked down at her hands to keep me from seeing the tears that were starting to come.

"I thought Ray and I were made for each other," she said. "He was so attentive when we were dating, but a few months after we got married things began to change. He started losing his temper for no good reason. In the last few years it has gotten worse. He is impatient with the children, but he focuses most of his anger on me. He constantly tells me how stupid I am and criticizes everything I do. I feel like a worthless failure because, no matter how hard I try, I can't make him happy."

Susan started listing all of the things that her husband was doing to make her feel bad about herself, but after listening for a few minutes I gently changed the subject and said something that helped her to begin the process of being a victor, not a victim. "Susan, you are basing your identity on what your husband says about you instead of finding your identity in Christ. Are you willing to allow the Lord to tell you who you are?"

Susan and I worked on this and several other mistakes she was making and, after a few weeks, she said that her whole perspective began to change. "I have been drawing closer to Jesus and, as I pray and study the Bible, I am finding out who I am—in Him," Susan said. Her eyes sparkled as she continued, "I spent the last ten years feeling like a failure for not being able to make my husband happy. I hungered for his approval so I could feel good about myself. But now I am beginning to find my identity in Christ, not my husband. I know that because I belong to Jesus, God loves me and approves of me, and that's what really matters most to me now."

Think About It

Susan based her identity on the approval (or disapproval) of her husband. In the passage surrounding Today's Verse, Paul warns us not to put our confidence in the flesh (base our identity on who we are or what we have done), like he used to do. Then he lists things on which he used to base his identity. Can you find them?

Philippians 3:4b–6— *"If anyone else thinks he has reasons to put confidence in the flesh, I have more: circumcised on the eighth day* [A ____], *of the people of Israel, of the tribe of Benjamin, a Hebrew of Hebrews* [B ____]; *in regard to the law, a Pharisee* [C ____]; *as for zeal, persecuting the church* [D ____]; *as for legalistic righteousness, faultless* [E ____]."

Place one of these numbers in the corresponding space (A–E) above:
1. Having an impressive job
2. Following religious traditions
3. Earning his standing with God by perfect obedience
4. Coming from a good family
5. Putting great energy into doing what he thought was right

Answers: A2, B4, C1, D5, E3

All of these things made Paul feel good about himself—they were to his profit—but after he met Jesus, he considered them all a loss. In Philippians 3:8 he says that he considers them rubbish *"compared to the surpassing greatness of knowing Christ Jesus my Lord."*

Check things that you consider profit (really important) in determining your identity:

☐ Appearance   ☐ Possessions   ☐ Money
☐ Profession   ☐ Power   ☐ Success
☐ Approval   ☐ Ability   ☐ Correctness
☐ Intelligence   ☐ Family

Which of these things make you feel good about yourself? Do you have an impressive job? Do you drop names or wear labels? Do you build big houses or get extra degrees? Do you flaunt your "perfect" children and hide your worries under a mask?

What makes you feel bad about yourself? Do you fret about being overweight? Are you embarrassed because your kids aren't walking with the Lord? Have regrets that you never found Mr. Right, or maybe because Mr. Right turned into Mr. Wrong?

Write About It

If you have a personal relationship with Jesus Christ as your Savior and Lord, who are you? In the first chapter, we talked about the fact we are God's beloved children. The following passages focus on who we are as a result of His love for us.

Place a check next to the verse that helps you most today.

What Happens When God Loves Me?

I am clean—righteous (right with God).	1 Corinthians 6:11b (NLT)— *"But now your sins have been washed away, and you have been set apart for God. You have been made right with God because of what the Lord Jesus Christ and the Spirit of our God have done for you."*
I am acceptable to God—pure, holy, and free.	1 Corinthians 1:30b (NLT)— *"He [Christ] is the one who made us acceptable to God. He made us pure and holy, and he gave himself to purchase our freedom."*
I am more than a conqueror.	Romans 8:37— *"No, in all these things we are more than conquerors through him who loved us."*

I am loved by God just as I am.	Romans 5:8— *"But God demonstrates his own love for us in this: While we were still sinners, Christ died for us."*
I stand next to Christ in a place of highest privilege.	Romans 5:2 (NLT)— *"Because of our faith, Christ has brought us into this place of highest privilege where we now stand, and we confidently and joyfully look forward to sharing God's glory."*
I have the power to turn from destructive vicious cycles that lead to sin.	Romans 8:2 (NLT)— *"For the power of the life-giving Spirit has freed you through Christ Jesus from the power of sin that leads to death."*
God is on my side.	Romans 8:31b— *"If God is for us, who can be against us?"*

Pray About It

Tell God about the verse above that helps you most and why it helps you today. Read this prayer as you think about Today's Verse, Philippians 3:7— *"But whatever was to my profit I now consider loss for the sake of Christ."*

Lord, I don't want to base my identity on what someone else thinks of me, rather than basing it on Your Word. But I have to admit that I find myself doing that at times. When people criticize me, help me to look to You and remember Whose I am. Help me stop trying to impress people so I will feel good about myself. When I stop to think about the fact that You know me and love me, how could I base my identity on anything as trivial as the criticisms or compliments of people around me? Thank You, Lord, that when I study Your Word and believe Your promises I can have confidence because of who I am in Christ.

Do It

Base your identity on this and nothing else: Jesus loves me, this I know!

Chapter 3

How Can I Leave My Unhealthy Ways Behind?

Day 11

Leaving Shame Behind

Today's Verse

Isaiah 54:4a— *"Do not be afraid; you will not suffer shame. Do not fear disgrace; you will not be humiliated. You will forget the shame of your youth."*

Read About It

I was sitting in the mall one afternoon waiting for a friend who was going to join me for lunch. While I waited, I noticed a little girl, about six, whose mother was screaming at her because she had spilled her drink. "You are always so clumsy!" the angry mother hissed. "I hate to take you places because you always embarrass me!" On and on the woman ranted. I looked at the sadness on the little girl's face and realized how hurt she was by her mother's caustic remarks.

Tears stung my eyes and I was surprised at how deeply I felt the little girl's pain. As I sat there, I realized that it wasn't just her pain I was feeling; it was my own. Watching this humiliating scene brought back the feelings of shame I experienced as a child. As I prayed for that little girl, I asked God to draw her close and comfort her—to help her to forget the shame of her youth just as He was helping me.

Think About It

> Shame is the feeling that something is fundamentally wrong with you. Guilt is feeling bad about what you have done. Shame is feeling bad about who you are.

Here are some other symptoms of shame. Place a check next to any symptoms you have:

☐ Shame makes you feel that you are not as good as other people. That thought hurts down deep even though you are often not aware of it.

☐ Shame encourages you to be embarrassed for things that are not your fault and to blame yourself for things you didn't cause.

☐ Shame constantly says that you are at its mercy and that there is no way out of its misery.

☐ Shame encourages you to wear a mask. It says, "If people really knew you, they wouldn't like you."

☐ Shame demands to be hidden. It knows that when it is brought out into the light, it becomes weaker.

☐ Shame encourages you to accept inferior relationships and disrespectful treatment.

Certain situations trigger shame. Here are some common shame triggers. Check ones that trigger your shame.

☐ Receiving criticism   ☐ Not fitting in with the crowd
☐ Experiencing conflict   ☐ Making a mistake
☐ Being made fun of   ☐ Other triggers:

Let me give you an example of one of my shame triggers. I realized a few years ago that losing things was a shame trigger for me. I have always been pretty scatterbrained and was shamed as a child every time I lost something, so as an adult I had a tendency to shame myself every time I lost anything. I would call myself "stupid" or "absentminded" and would feel hopeless and disgusted with myself. Once I realized that losing things was a shame trigger, I found that my shame disappeared if I prayed out loud while I looked for the lost item—thanking God that He loved me and was helping me.

You may attempt to do good things to cover up your shame and work very hard to heal the humiliation you feel inside. Place a check next to any of the following that you feel driven to do:

☐ Be successful   ☐ Make people like you
☐ Be attractive and/or thin   ☐ Say only the things you
☐ Be powerful   think others want you to say
☐ Have a lot of money   ☐ Do things perfectly

Another way people cover up their shame is by denying it. People deny the shame they feel in different ways. Check ways that apply to you:

☐ Some deny shame by refusing to feel anything. They go through life denying their emotions and negative thoughts.
☐ Some deny shame by acting in a shameless manner.
☐ Some deny shame by focusing on the shame of others.
☐ Some deny shame by following rigid rules. They ignore the gospel message of grace and focus on earning their salvation.
☐ Some deny shame by compulsive behavior. A compulsive behavior is anything that you can't stop doing even though it is causing problems in your life.

Here are some of the most common compulsive behaviors (or addictions). Circle any compulsive behaviors that you have.

Overeating	Sex	TV
Drinking	Work	Fixing others'
Drugs	Internet	problems
Spending money	Sports	Controlling others
Other:		

Write About It ✐

Many of us have a deep sense of shame. The exciting thing is that shame can be defeated! The Bible tells us clearly how to cooperate with the Lord as He removes our shame. We will talk about this today and tomorrow.

Psalm 32:5 gives us the first step in this process: *"Then I acknowledged my sin to you and did not cover up my iniquity. I said, 'I will confess my transgressions to the LORD'—and you forgave the guilt of my sin."* List the things you have done that have contributed to your shame. Keep Psalm 32:5 in mind as you make this list. Don't cover up anything, and remember that God will forgive everything. Continue on another page if necessary.

1. _____
2. _____
3. _____
4. _____

Pray, telling God that you are sorry for doing these things and thanking Him for sending Jesus to pay the price for your sins.

List things that have been done to you that have contributed to your shame. Include things such as abuse, unfair treatment, ridicule, and neglect.

1. _____
2. _____

3. _____
4. _____

Ask God to help you to forgive those who have contributed to your shame. We will discuss more about how to forgive in just a few days. The way to start is to pray for willingness to forgive those who have hurt you, even when they don't deserve it.

List circumstances that made you feel ashamed. Include things such as having an alcoholic parent or being poor, handicapped, or overweight.

1. _____
2. _____
3. _____
4. _____

James 5:16a gives us the second step in the process of recovering from shame: *"Therefore confess your sins to each other and pray for each other that you may be healed."* Pray that God will bring to mind the name of a Christian whom you can trust to talk to about these things. Be sure this person is one who can keep a confidence and has a good understanding of God's grace and forgiveness. Do you know the person you will talk to? If so, write his or her name here:

_____

In His Word, God says this to you: No matter what you have done, no matter what you have become, no matter what has been done to you, bring me your shame and your guilt and let me heal you. I sent my Son to die for your sins and take away your shame. Accept the grace I offer you today.

Consider making an appointment now so that you won't put it off. I believe that you will be amazed to see how sharing these things with God and another person helps to free you of the shame you feel.

Pray About It

Pray as you consider Today's Verse. Isaiah 54:4a— *"Do not be afraid; you will not suffer shame. Do not fear disgrace; you will not be humiliated. You will forget the shame of your youth."*

Father, thank You so much that You are helping me to forget my shame—the shameful things that I have done and things that have been done to me. Help me not to be afraid to acknowledge these things to You and to tell a trusted Christian as well. Help me to bring my shame out into Your light and cooperate with You as You set me free from it.

Do It

Shame hates to be called by name. It loses its strength when you tell someone. Talk to a trusted Christian friend today!

Day 12
Leaving Excuses Behind

Today's Verse

Proverbs 13:18— *"He who ignores discipline comes to poverty and shame, but whoever heeds correction is honored."*

Read About It 📖

It happened when I was working in an ICU in a hospital in Texas. I had just purchased a beautiful new uniform. Although I was overweight, I still tried to look my best and spent hours trying to find clothes that didn't make me "look fat." That night, one of the doctors greeted me in front of several of the staff with an enthusiastic "Congratulations!" I couldn't think of anything outstanding I had done lately, so I asked expectantly, "For what?" The doctor answered innocently, "For your pregnancy. You are going to have a baby, aren't you?"

If you're overweight you will understand the horror I experienced, as I muttered a quiet, "No, I guess this new uniform isn't very becoming." Dying of shame, I quickly busied myself taking care of one of the patients, swearing that I would eat no more than 500 calories a day until I weighed 100 pounds. Then I went home and did something unimaginable: I binged until I was sick. I excused it with a frustrated, "I can't help it."

I didn't understand why I ate so uncontrollably then, but I do now. When people feel ashamed, they feel overwhelmed with hopelessness. They often feel so disgusted with themselves that they give up and do the very things that will add to their shame. They don't mean to ignore discipline and they want to heed correction, but they don't know how.

Think About It 💡

Can you identify with what I said about doing the very thing that will contribute to your shame? When I asked a woman I was counseling, Pat, that question, she answered with a definite "YES!" She said, "I told you how my father shamed me as a child by screaming at me. The amazing thing is that I did almost the same thing to my son—even though that's the last thing I wanted to do. I found it impossible to control my temper, and I treated my son almost like my father had treated me."

Here are three other examples of people who repeated the shameful things done to them:

• Joe was ashamed because he had an alcoholic father, but he became an alcoholic himself.

• Susan was ashamed because she had an obese mother, but she eventually became obese herself.

• Mary hated the fact that her mother kept such a messy house, but when she grew up, she did too.

Fortunately, all five of us stopped contributing to our shame when we quit ignoring the Lord's discipline and began heeding His direction. Let me help you to begin doing these two things so that God will break the cycle of shame in your life.

Write About It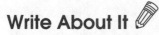

How are you contributing to your shame?

_____

What are you doing that made you ashamed when it was done to you (or around you) as a child?

_____

Let's look again at the two commands in Today's Verse:

1. Quit ignoring discipline: Stop ignoring the consequences that are occurring because you continue to do these things. Ask yourself this question: How is doing the things I listed above hurting me?

Now ask yourself another question: How is doing these things helping me? We don't continue to do things that don't help us in some way or another—so what you are doing must "help" you in some way. Let me explain by using the examples I gave you earlier:

Thing we were doing	How it hurt us	How it helped us
I was overeating	I had bad health, shame, no energy	It numbed my feelings, distracted me
Pat was screaming at her son	Pat hurt her son, hated herself	She got her way; it seemed easier
Mary was keeping a messy house	The mess made Mary miserable; she couldn't find things	She could be lazy; it seemed easier

Fill in the blank spaces below with your own answers. In the left column list things you are doing that add to your shame. Then in the other two columns, list several ways each one helps you and hurts you.

Thing that I am doing	How it hurts me	How it helps me

When you realize that these things hurt you more than they help you, you will be encouraged to quit ignoring discipline.

2. Heed God's correction: The Holy Spirit tells you about the things you are doing that cause you to feel ashamed. So what is keeping you from heeding God's correction? *Excuses* are!

Let's look at excuses that you use that "give yourself permission" to do these things which contribute to your shame. Here are the most common excuses. Place a check next to the excuses that you use and list others that you make.

____1. I can't help it.

____2. I can't do it.

____3. I'm too busy.

____4. It's their fault.

5. _____

6. _____

Place the promise that God gives you next to the corresponding excuse above:

A. In 2 Corinthians 9:8, God tells you that He will give you the power to do anything that He commands you to do.

B. In Matthew 7:5, Jesus tells you to examine your own faults before looking at someone else's.

C. In 1 Corinthians 10:13, God promises not to give you a temptation that you can't stand up against.

D. In Matthew 6:33, Jesus tells you to put God and His righteousness first.

Answers: 1C, 2A, 3D, 4B

Pray About It

Reflect on Today's Verse as you ask God to help you to quit ignoring discipline (recognize how your actions are harming you and others) and heed His correction (quit making excuses). Proverbs 13:18— *"He who ignores discipline comes to poverty and shame, but whoever heeds correction is honored."*

Lord, thank You that, by Your grace, I can do everything that You want me to do—even things that in my own strength would be impossible. I know that if I ignore Your discipline and refuse to heed Your correction, I will continue in my cycle of shame. My shame will grow and affect my loved ones as well. Help me to listen to what You are telling me in Today's Verse—to see how my wrong choices are harming me and to leave my old ways behind me.

Do It

Ignoring discipline hurts you more than it helps you...so quit!

Day 13
Leaving Grumbling Behind

Today's Verse

Psalm 130:1 *(NLT)—* "From the depths of
despair, O LORD, I call for your help."

Read About It

I used to be a grumbler. When things didn't go my way, I
said so to just about anyone who wanted to listen, and many
who didn't. Somehow, I believed that dumping my problems
on others made my load lighter. I also believed that it
excused me from responsibility because my problems were
always someone else's fault. After years of grumbling, I
finally began to see what it was doing to me and my family,
so I started crying out to the Lord for help. When I became
willing to accept His help, God began changing me. I can
truthfully say that I am an ex-grumbler and it is wonderful to
be free of that horrible habit!

Think About It

We have many examples of grumblers in the Bible. Probably
the most famous group of grumblers is the Israelites while
they were being led out of Egypt. Psalm 106:24–25 (NLT) tells
us about them: *"The people refused to enter the pleasant land,
for they wouldn't believe his promise to care for them. Instead,
they grumbled in their tents."*

That's the way many of us are. We refuse to enter the
pleasant land because we won't believe God's promise to
care for us. We miss out on many of the blessings God has
for us because we're stuck in our tents, grumbling.

Let's look at another grumbler. You probably remember Jesus' parable of the prodigal son. The younger son got his inheritance early and squandered it. When he was destitute, he came home to his father, who welcomed him with open arms. The prodigal son had actively rebelled against his father, but the father forgave him and threw a party when he returned. I imagine that the older brother grumbled to himself for years, but he finally let it come out when he heard about his brother's party. Read Luke 15:28–31 to see what he said.

Match the symptoms of a grumbler with the response of the older brother.

Symptoms of a grumbler:
_____ 1. Ineffective communication
_____ 2. Exaggeration
_____ 3. Blame/jealousy
_____ 4. Ingratitude

How the older brother shows that he is a grumbler—place the letter of one of the following after the matching symptom above:
A. "I've been slaving for you…" "I never disobeyed you…"
B. "My son," the father said, "you are always with me, and everything I have is yours."
C. The older brother has been hurt all this time and never came to his father to discuss it.
D. "But when this son of yours who has squandered your property with prostitutes comes home, you kill the fattened calf for him!"

Answers: 1C, 2A, 3D, 4B

Write About It 🖉

It is easy for us to recognize the quality of grumbling in

someone else, but very difficult to recognize it in ourselves. Write the name of someone you know who is a grumbler. _____ Think about how much you enjoy listening as this person dumps his or her complaints on you. Now answer these questions to see if you also have a problem with grumbling.

Are You a Grumbler?

Yes___ No___ 1. Do you frequently grumble about your circumstances either in secret or out loud?

Yes___ No___ 2. Do you often forget to thank God when He blesses you?

Yes___ No___ 3. Are you so focused on what you don't have that you don't enjoy what you do have?

Yes___ No___ 4. Do you often blame others for your problems?

Yes___ No___ 5. Do you enjoy having people feel sorry for you?

Yes___ No___ 6. Do you often get upset when someone less deserving than you receives favor?

If you have two or more *yes* answers, your habit of complaining may be getting in your way. If you have identified this problem, rejoice because now you can do something about it! Admitting a problem is half of the solution. Here are some ways to quit being a grumbler.

1. Whenever you are upset, instead of dumping your stress on someone else, call out for God's help. Today's Verse reminds us to call out for God's help. It may be more effective to write your prayers because you will be able to focus on what you are really feeling. Often while you are writing your prayers, the Lord will bring to mind a solution— something positive that you can do to help the situation. If He doesn't, ask Him.

2. Determine not to ruin your day by grumbling. Psalm 118:24— *"This is the day the LORD has made; let us rejoice and be glad in it."* When you are tempted to grumble, remember that this will take away your joy. You find joy only when you abide in the Lord (John 15:4), and you can't do that when you are grumbling.

3. Every morning and whenever you are faced with a temptation to grumble, pray that God will help you to guard your words. Psalm 141:3— *"Set a guard over my mouth, O LORD; keep watch over the door of my lips."* Realize how serious grumbling can be. The Bible tells us that our words can turn our lives into *"a blazing flame of destruction"* (James 3:6 NLT).

4. Get together each week with a prayer partner and share things that upset you. Ecclesiastes 4:9–10 (NLT)— *"Two people can accomplish more than twice as much as one; they get a better return for their labor. If one person falls, the other can reach out and help. But people who are alone when they fall are in real trouble."* Share your problems with your prayer partner, but do not dump them on him or her. Here are some suggestions to help you do this:
• Spend a few minutes preparing for your meeting by writing a prayer about why you are upset (refer to #1 above).
• Choose a few of the most important paragraphs.
• Read this to your prayer partner.
• Don't have a grumbling attitude when you talk to your prayer partner; instead, share your problems so that your partner can give you another perspective and pray for you.

5. Each morning confess to the Lord any grumbling you did the day before. Psalm 32:5a— *"Then I acknowledged my sin to you and did not cover up my iniquity."* Rejoice that when you confess your sins, God forgives you (1 John 1:9), but be aware that He doesn't excuse you from the consequences that your grumbling causes. We have discussed several consequences of a grumbling attitude. Check the ones you are experiencing. Can you think of others?

• I have missed out on many blessings.
• I have remained stuck in my problems.
• I have lost my joy.
• God has disciplined me.
• I have been a bad influence on others.
• People don't want to be around me.

You're paying a big price for grumbling. Is it worth it?

Consider what others have said about grumbling.
"Complaining about our lot in life might seem quite innocent in itself, but God takes it personally."
—Erwin W. Lutzer (1941–)

"Some people are always grumbling because roses have thorns; I am thankful that thorns have roses."
—Alphonse Karr (1808–1890)

"When we are discontented with ourselves, we complain about others."
—Paul Tournier (1898–1986)

"It isn't your problems that are bothering you. It is the way you are looking at them."
—Epictetus (c.55–c.135)

Pray About It

Reflect on Today's Verse as you ask God to help you quit grumbling. Psalm 130:1 (NLT)— *"From the depths of despair, O LORD, I call for your help."*

Please help me to bring my cares to You, Lord. Help me not to grumble and have a negative attitude like the Israelites or the prodigal's older brother. Even when my circumstances are difficult, help me to have a thankful heart. Help me to praise You because You are taking care of me, helping me with my problems, and giving me joy even in the midst of them.

Do It

When you dump your problems on someone else, you might feel better temporarily, but the other person sure doesn't! Cast your cares on the Lord instead.

Day 14
Leaving Regret Behind

Today's Verse

Joel 2:25a (KJV)— "*And I will restore to you the years that the locust hath eaten.*"

Read About It

"My husband left me," Susanne said in a daze as she arrived for her counseling appointment. Her blue eyes were bloodshot and puffy. "Look at what a mess I have made of my life! I have nothing left to live for." Susanne was devastated. Just last week, we had talked about how her husband seemed angry all the time and was away from home almost every evening. This week he told her that he was in love with another woman, packed a few things, and left.

"I shouldn't have ever married him," Susanne mourned. "I knew that he was married when we started dating, but he and his wife hadn't been getting along for a long time, and I thought…" Susanne couldn't finish her sentence because of her uncontrollable sobbing. I comforted her while she cried, and when she was finally able to speak she said, "I wasted ten years in that marriage and I have ruined my life."

I told her about God's amazing promise in Today's Verse and we started talking about ways she could draw closer to the Lord. She tearfully told Him about all of the hurt she was experiencing and confessed the sins she had committed along the way. Then Susanne asked God to help her to let go of regrets so she could let Him rebuild her life—to restore the years the locusts had eaten.

God kept His promise. In the year since her husband left, Susanne has been growing spiritually by leaps and bounds. She leads a divorce recovery group in her church and told me the other day: "I am starting to feel like a whole person for the first time in my life." Susanne said joyfully, "God has restored my life, but now it's even better, and God is using the years I thought were wasted to prepare me to help others."

Think About It

Have you ever seen a locust? I remember seeing some when I was a little girl. They were everywhere, and it was hard to walk without stepping on one and hearing a yucky crunching sound under my feet. But that was nothing compared to the plagues of locusts that have devastated crops in many parts of the world. Swarms of migrating locusts are sometimes so large that they make every aspect of living difficult. They are so thick that they can block out the sunlight, and they eat up everything in sight—causing famine, economic ruin, and unimaginable catastrophes.

You probably remember the plague of locusts that God sent to convince Pharaoh to let the Israelites leave Egypt. Read the graphic description in Exodus 10:15 of what locusts can do— *"They covered all the ground until it was black. They devoured all that was left after the hail—everything growing in the fields and the fruit on the trees. Nothing green remained on tree or plant in all the land of Egypt."*

Write About It ✏

Have "locusts" stripped your life of good things like they did Susanne's? No matter where you turn, are you reminded of what you lost and what might have been? Are you living in gloom and darkness because of something you did or something that was done to you? If so, cling to Today's Verse and God's promise to restore the years the locusts have eaten.

There have been many locusts in my life, but the most significant was my inability to stop overeating. What are the locusts in your life? Place a check next to ones that have affected you.

☐ Childhood abuse   ☐ The death of a loved one
☐ Sickness   ☐ Natural disaster
☐ Rejection   ☐ Poverty
☐ Ridicule   ☐ Inability
☐ Mistakes

My overeating caused me to become overweight and get involved in a cycle of shame that took over 30 years to break. What effect have these locusts had on you?

☐ Depression   ☐ Shame
☐ Loneliness   ☐ Hopelessness
☐ Self-pity   ☐ Anger
☐ Emptiness   ☐ Feeling separated from God

Write a few sentences about the years your locusts have eaten.

_____

_____

_____

_____

_____

God has promised to restore the years the locusts have eaten. He has done that in my life by turning my misery to ministry. Without my problem with food and the misery it caused, I wouldn't be a lay counselor, I wouldn't have a ministry helping people to lose weight; I wouldn't have written numerous books or have the opportunity to speak across the country telling people about the Lord.

God will restore the years your locusts have eaten, but you must cooperate with Him in this process. You just did the first two things that open the way for God's restoration:

1. Recognize the locusts in your life.

2. Recognize the effect the locusts have had on you.

Now continue to cooperate with the Lord by following the commands that go with the wonderful promise we have been talking about in Today's Verse.

3. Joel 2:13a (KJV)— *"And rend your heart, and not your garments..."* The word "rend" means to tear something as a sign of grief or despair. In Old Testament times it was a custom to tear your clothing to show grief. But God says to rend your heart instead of your garments. This means that He wants you to let your heart be broken—to grieve the locusts in your life in a deep way.

Tell God all about the pain and disappointment your locusts have caused. Take responsibility if you played a part in the locusts' devastation, and confess this to Him as well. If you feel angry with God for allowing your locusts, tell Him and ask Him to help you.

4. Joel 2:13b (KJV)— *"and turn unto the LORD your God..."* As you turn to the Lord and bring Him your broken heart, He will help you to let go of regret over the locusts in your life. **When you let go, you let God's restoration begin.** Write a prayer of letting go and letting God.

_____

_____

_____

_____

5. Look at the other wonderful promises of restoration that God gives to those who obey the commands we just talked about. Joel 2:26 gives us three promises.

Promise #1: *"You will have plenty to eat, until you are full."* (You will no longer feel empty; instead you will feel a delightful sense of satisfaction.)

Promise #2: *"You will praise the name of the LORD your God, who has worked wonders for you."* (You will praise God when you see how wonderfully He has worked everything out.)

Promise #3: *"Never again will my people be shamed."* (You will never have to live in shame again.)

Pray About It 🙏

Pray as you focus on Today's Verse, Joel 2:25a (KJV)— *"And I will restore to you the years that the locust hath eaten."*

Lord, thank You that I don't have to remain stuck in regret over the locusts in my life and the years they have eaten. I praise You for Your promise of restoration. You tell me that You will restore the years the locusts have eaten, but I know that I won't receive Your restoration unless I obey the commands that go with the promise. Help me to rend my heart— to deeply confess my sins and grief, and bring my broken heart to You.

Do It 🦶

Let go of your regrets and let God restore the years the locusts have eaten.

Day 15
Leaving Unforgiveness Behind

Today's Verse

1 John 2:11— "But whoever hates his brother is in the darkness and walks around in the darkness; he does not know where he is going, because the darkness has blinded him."

Read About It

Kathy, an attractive mother of two, came to me for counseling because she felt worn out all the time. She had been feeling exhausted for several years and hopelessly stuck—unable to go forward because she was always so tired. Doctor's tests revealed nothing that would explain her extreme fatigue. But after talking to Kathy, I saw something that might be consuming her energy. Kathy was holding on to unforgiveness.

Kathy's mother had always been very critical of her, and Kathy spent most of her childhood desperately trying to please her. "She blew up at me for everything, and I never knew when she would explode," Kathy mourned. After listening to the list of other things her mother had done, I gently encouraged Kathy to pray for willingness to forgive her mother, but her response was understandable: Kathy said bitterly, "My mother doesn't deserve it."

My heart went out to her and I replied, "I can only imagine how much your mother has hurt you. But there's an old saying: 'Hurting people hurt people.' The person you are hurting is yourself." I could see from Kathy's eyes that my words made sense, and I took her hand and said softly, "Will you let me show you how to rely on God to help you forgive your mother?" She said a quiet "yes," and we started on the journey that eventually led to Kathy's freedom from the

exhausting burden of unforgiveness and a new life full of joy
and vitality.

Pay special attention to the next two sessions if you haven't
been able to forgive someone, even if the offense seems
unimportant or it happened long ago. Today we will focus
on the importance of forgiveness, and tomorrow we will discuss how to forgive. Mark this section in your book so that
you can find it later. I'm sure you'll have opportunities to use
it again.

When we talk about people we need to forgive, who comes
to your mind? _____

Think About It

The Bible is full of word pictures that draw vivid images to
show what can happen if we let unforgiveness (and its close
friends—blaming, judging, and criticizing) into our lives. Let's
look at some of them, starting with another look at Today's
Verse. While you're looking at these verses, I want to ask you
to do something that will really help you to understand them
in a deeper way: On a separate sheet of paper, draw a stick-
figure cartoon of each of these word pictures.

An Unforgiving Person Is Like...
A blind person stumbling around: 1 John 2:11— *"But
whoever hates his brother is in the darkness and walks
around in the darkness; he does not know where he is going,
because the darkness has blinded him."*
Someone who has given the devil a foothold: Ephesians
4:26–27— *"'In your anger do not sin': Do not let the sun go
down while you are still angry, and do not give the devil a
foothold."*
Someone with a plank in his eye: Luke 6:41— *"Why do
you look at the speck of sawdust in your brother's eye and pay
no attention to the plank in your own eye?"*

A woman who tears her own house down: Proverbs 14:1— *"The wise woman builds her house, but with her own hands the foolish one tears hers down."*

Someone in prison being tortured: Matthew 18:32–34— *"Then the master called the servant in. 'You wicked servant,' he said, 'I canceled all that debt of yours because you begged me to. Shouldn't you have had mercy on your fellow servant just as I had on you?' In anger his master turned him over to the jailers to be tortured, until he should pay back all he owed."*

Write About It ✎

Look again at Today's Verse, noting the harmful things that can happen when someone holds on to unforgiveness. Have you been blind to the harm of unforgiveness? Which of these symptoms are you experiencing?

• Frequent illnesses. Unforgiveness causes stress that can lower your immune system so you are more open to things like colds, viruses, and even conditions such as cancer. And it can cause other serious physical problems, such as ulcers, high blood pressure, strokes, and heart attacks.

• Depression. When unforgiveness lingers, it can lead to a constant state of depression.

• Fatigue, insomnia. When you don't forgive someone it can be as exhausting as carrying that person around on your back day and night.

• Overeating and other addictions. Many people turn to addictions to numb the pain unforgiveness causes.

• Acting in unbecoming ways. People sometimes literally waste their lives trying to get even with someone who has offended them, and their payback is a paradox: they often become like the one that they hate.

Ephesians 4:26–27 teaches us: *"In your anger do not sin': Do not let the sun go down while you are still angry, and do not give the devil a foothold."* Anger is not always sinful, but it is when we react in sinful ways. What are some ways people sin in their anger? Circle ones that apply to you.

• Holding on to anger, unwilling to forgive, becoming resentful and bitter
• Saying hurtful things, ridiculing, being sarcastic
• Responding with rage, physical violence, threats, vengeance
• Gossiping, judging, criticizing, having unrealistic expectations
• Withholding love
• Feeling self-righteous, putting someone down to build yourself up
• Other _____

Luke 6:41 asks, *"Why do you look at the speck of sawdust in your brother's eye and pay no attention to the plank in your own eye?"* Do you play the Blame Game—criticizing others' faults while ignoring your own? Yes___ No___

Proverbs 14:1 has a word for women: *"The wise woman builds her house, but with her own hands the foolish one tears hers down."* Do you tear your own house down? Write ways that you are tearing your own house down.

_____
_____
_____
_____
_____

Matthew 18:32–34: *"Then the master called the servant in. 'You wicked servant,' he said, 'I canceled all that debt of yours because you begged me to. Shouldn't you have had mercy on your fellow servant just as I had on you?' In anger his master turned him over to the jailers to be tortured, until he should pay back all he owed."*

Yes___ No___ Are negative feelings making you miserable?
Yes___ No___ Do you feel like you're in prison—unable to get free so you can get on with your life?
Yes___ No___ Are you unable to feel forgiven by the Lord for the things that you have done?

Pray About It

Review the word pictures and your answers in the Write About It section concerning the harm that unforgiveness can do. Pray, confessing any unforgiveness that you have—even if it seems insignificant—and ask God for His help.

Lord, when Jesus told the disciples that they needed to forgive seventy times seven times, they cried in dismay, "Increase our faith!" I say the same thing to You today. There is no way for me to forgive some of the things that people have done to me. But since You never command me to do anything that You won't empower me to do, I can say with confidence, "I can do all things through Christ—even forgive the unforgivable." Help me to cooperate with You in the process of forgiveness by recognizing it, confessing it to You, and relying on Your grace to give me the desire and ability to forgive.

Do It

Don't stay stuck in unforgiveness and the misery it brings, or you won't be able to step forward to the joy and freedom that await you!

Chapter 4

How Can I Do Better?

Day 16

Learning to Forgive

Today's Verse

Luke 6:28— [Jesus said] *"Bless those who curse you, pray for those who mistreat you."*

Read About It

Susan was raped when she was 14, and her young life seemed ruined. Several years after the incident, when she told her pastor about the hatred she felt toward the rapist, he gently shared Today's Verse with her. He encouraged Susan to forgive the man—not because he deserved it, but because forgiveness was the only way to be free of the harm he caused her.

"The way to begin the process of forgiveness is by praying for him every day," her pastor said. Susan hesitantly agreed to do it. At first, she prayed without feeling, through gritted teeth. But through the months that followed, with the help of a Christian counselor, she prayed faithfully every day for the man who raped her. After a while, her heart began to soften a little and spontaneous prayers for the man began to pour forth from her. She prayed that God would bless him by sending godly people to minister to him. And she asked God to heal the hurts in the man that caused him to be so hurtful to others. One day, as Susan prayed for the man who had harmed her in such a terrible way, she was amazed to discover that her rage had been replaced by pity.

Susan was 40 when she told me about her rape. She had never forgotten that traumatic event, but it no longer haunted her. She told me how she had become active as a volunteer in a rape crisis center, and she beamed when she said that she had shared Christ with many women who came to her there. God had taken the terrible harm done to her and used it for good in her own life and in the lives of countless others because she was willing to obey Jesus' commands in Today's Verse. When she prayed for her rapist, she opened up the way for God's power to work in her, so that through His grace, she was able to forgive—even the unforgivable.

Think About It

In addition to prayer, we can do other practical things that will help us to forgive.

1. Get rid of misconceptions about forgiveness. Here are some of the most common ones. Check any misconceptions that you have believed.

☐ It is impossible for me to forgive. **The truth is:** God's grace empowers me to forgive.

☐ I don't have to forgive because the person doesn't deserve it. **The truth is:** God commands me to forgive. I don't deserve God's forgiveness, but He forgives me. And when I forgive, God sets me free from the destruction that unforgiveness can bring.

☐ I only feel worse when I think about what I need to forgive, so I'm better off putting it on the back burner. **The**

truth is: Just like a pot left simmering on the back burner of my stove, if I put anger on the back burner of my mind without dealing with it, it will char my soul.

☐ I must confront the one who hurt me, and they must apologize and change before I can forgive him or her. **The truth is:** Forgiveness is a choice I can make when I rely on God to help me one day at a time. This process does not depend on the other person.

☐ If I forgive the person, it is as if I am giving them permission to continue to hurt me. **The truth is:** Forgiveness does not mean that I have to continue to submit myself to mistreatment. God commands me to forgive, but He does not want me to repeat harmful patterns.

☐ If I haven't forgotten about my hurt, I haven't forgiven. **The truth is:** The hurts of my past may continue to come to mind, but it is what I do with them that is important. Every time I remember an offense, I need to take it to the Lord and refuse to nurse a grudge or cherish a hurt.

Another thing that will help you to forgive is to get rid of misconceptions about how to "bless those who curse you." Here are some of the most common ones. Check misconceptions you have believed.

☐ I bless people by allowing them to treat me in an unkind way. **The truth is:** I bless people by not enabling their unkind behavior. For example, Mary says to a family member, "When you scream at me like that, I'm leaving the room. I'll discuss this with you when you are calmer."

☐ I bless people by protecting them from consequences of their behavior. **The truth is:** Often, the best way to bless people is by allowing them to receive the consequences that result from their behavior. For example, Sue, the wife of an alcoholic, refuses to lie to his boss about why he is not coming to work.

☐ I bless volatile people by placating them so they won't blow up at me. **The truth is:** We are to act out of love, not fear. Often, the best way to bless a volatile person is by standing up courageously in the face of his or her anger.

☐ I bless people by saying only things that they want to hear. **The truth is:** Often, the best way to bless people is to care enough to confront them and tell them the truth in love. This must be done with prayer.

Other practical things that will help us to forgive...

Empathetic repentance. When you are thinking about criticizing someone else, ask yourself this question: "How do I do the same thing or something similar?" This encourages us to put Luke 6:41 into action. (*"Why do you look at the speck of sawdust in your brother's eye and pay no attention to the plank in your own eye?"*)

Quit trying to change others. We cannot change anyone else. That is God's job. If you are angry, ask yourself if you're trying to change the other person. If you are, confess this, and get busy asking God to change things in you that need changing.

Reach out for help. If you are constantly dealing with someone who hurts you, talk to a counselor, pastor, or trusted Christian friend.

Write About It ✏

Another important thing that will help you forgive is to write about your hurts. Think of the person you need to forgive most.

Follow this format on a separate sheet of paper (copied with permission from Sarah Morris, M.Ed., Family Therapist). This will help you in exciting ways, even if the person you write about has died. Write the same number of things under each item. For example, if you write three reasons you are angry, write three answers under the other items.

Write About Your Hurts

Write about why you are angry with this person:

1. _____

2. _____

3. _____

Write about the hurt they have caused you:

1. _____

2. _____

3. _____

Write about your fears or worries:

1. _____

2. _____

3. _____

Write about your regrets or things you wish you had done:

1. _____

2. _____

3. _____

Write about your love, caring, and/or the good times:

1. _____

2. _____

3. _____

Pray About It

Reflect on Today's Verse as you ask God to help you to forgive the person you most need to forgive. Luke 6:28— [Jesus said] *"Bless those who curse you, pray for those who mistreat you."*

A Prayer for Someone Who Has Hurt Me

Father, I pray for_____, who has hurt me so deeply. I pray that You will draw him (or her) to Yourself and help him to know You in a deeper way, through Christ. I pray that You will send godly people into his life to encourage him in his walk with You. Help him to trust You and hear Your voice. Bless him physically—that he may be in good health. Heal him of any physical problems. Bless him emotionally. Heal him of hurts he has experienced. Help him not to be overwhelmed by worries. I pray that You will shower him with Your blessings. And I pray that You will give him Your joy and peace.

Do It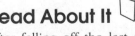

Let God heal your hurts so you won't be among the hurting people who are hurting people.

Day 17
Denying Myself

Today's Verse

Luke 9:23— *"Then he [Jesus] said to them all: 'If anyone would come after me, he must deny himself and take up his cross daily and follow me.'"*

Read About It

After falling off the last of a thousand diets, I asked myself the question that I should have asked years earlier: Are diets working for you?

I had been dieting since I could remember. I think I started when I was about eight. I would starve myself for days or months, only to regain all my weight, plus some. Inevitably, I would do fine until something stressful happened and I would fall off my diet. It worked the same way every time, but I never stopped to think about it. I just kept looking for a better diet that would carry me to some magical place where I would never have problems with overeating again. I was stuck in a vicious cycle. My *self* was helping it spin—Self-pity said, "Poor Julie. It's so difficult for you to lose weight." Self-consciousness and self-centeredness chimed in, saying, "Everyone thinks of little else except how much you weigh."

Finally, in 1982, I realized that the happily-ever-after diet I had been searching for didn't exist. As I applied Today's Verse to my problem, I determined that, one day at a time, I would lay down my "perfect diet," pick up my cross (my weakness with food), quit focusing on myself...and follow Jesus.

I was excited to discover that as I put my energy into following Jesus, He began to lead me out of the horrible diet mentality that had been consuming my thoughts. And He also began leading me out of wrong thinking that kept my focus on my *self* instead of Him. (To learn more about the Christian weight-loss program that evolved out of my struggles with overeating, check out my website www.stepforwarddiet.com.)

Think About It

Self-centered...self-conscious...self-pity...self-righteous...self-ish. In Today's Verse, Jesus tells us that if we want to come after Him, we must deny our *selves*. It doesn't matter which disease of self we have, whether we think we're too good (self-righteous) or too bad (self-conscious); all of them bring disease in our lives because they cause us to keep our eyes off of Jesus and on our selves. So the question is: How do we deny our *selves?* Jesus tells us in Today's Verse. He says to pick up our cross daily—to die to self one day at a time.

Let's look at some Scriptures that explain the concept of dying to self.
In the space provided next to each of these verses, write the letter of the corresponding idea found under How to Die to Self. (Parts of each passage are highlighted to give you some helpful hints.)

_____ 1. *"I have been crucified with Christ and I no longer live, but Christ lives in me. The life I live in the body, **I live by faith** in the Son of God, who loved me and gave himself for me."* —Galatians 2:20

_____ 2. *"For we know that our old self was crucified with him so that the body of sin might be done away with, that we should no longer be **slaves to sin**—because anyone who has died has been freed from sin."* —Romans 6:6–7

_____ 3. *"You were taught, with regard to your former way of life, to **put off your old self**, which is being corrupted by its deceitful desires; to be made new in the attitude of your minds; and to put on the new self, created to be like God in true righteousness and holiness."* —Ephesians 4:22–24

_____ 4. *"Since you have been raised to new life with Christ, set your sights on the realities of heaven, where Christ sits at God's right hand in the place of honor and power. **Let heaven fill your thoughts.** Do not think only about things down here on earth."* —Colossians 3:1–2 (NLT)

_____ 5. [Jesus said] *"For whoever wants to save his life will lose it, **but whoever loses his life for me will save it.** What good is it for a man to gain the whole world, and yet lose or forfeit his very self?"* —Luke 9:24–25

_____ 6. *"Your beauty should not come from outward adornment, such as braided hair and the wearing of gold jewelry and fine clothes. Instead, it should be that of your inner self, **the unfading beauty of a gentle** *and quiet spirit, which is of great worth in God's sight."* —1 Peter 3:3–4

How to Die to Self

A. Changing my attitude so I can put off my old sinful self and put on a new self, which is like Jesus.

B. Living by faith in Jesus—rejoicing in His love and relying on His help.

C. Remembering that I am no longer a slave to sin and that I have the freedom to choose whether to sin or not.

D. Knowing that I won't be beautiful in God's sight if I focus only on superficial things like my appearance.

E. Having a more heavenly perspective.

F. Giving up my will so I can do things God's way—knowing that by giving up what I want I will receive far more.

Answers: 1B, 2C, 3A, 4E, 5F, 6D

Write About It

How do you need to die to self? Answer the following questions.

I need to...

1. Change my attitude about _____

2. Put off my old sinful self. **What three things would you like to get rid of?**

_____

3. Put on my new self. **What new qualities would you like to have?**

_____

4. Live by faith in Jesus—rejoicing in His love and relying on His help. **In which area do you need His help most?**

_____

5. Remember that I am no longer a slave to sin and that I have the freedom to choose whether to sin or not. **What comes to mind when you read that you are no longer a slave to sin?** _____

6. Give up my will so I can do things God's way. **What comes to mind when you think about giving up your will?** _____

What Is a Cross?
A cross is a painful or challenging situation that you haven't caused and can't control. It is something that you have to face almost every day. To deal with it in a godly way, you must die to self. Here are some crosses.
• Chronic illness (yours or a family member's)
• Limited income
• A rebellious child
• Death of a loved one
• A difficult person
• A hard job
• Childhood abuse
• An unwanted divorce
• A disability (yours or a family member's)

What is a cross you have to bear? _____

Having identified a cross that we have to bear, we must be careful not to act like a martyr, complain, or feel sorry for ourselves. Instead, we determine to willingly pick up our crosses every day with a positive attitude and look for ways that the Lord is using it in our lives.

Pray About It

As you focus on Today's Verse, ask God to help you to deny your*self*, take up your cross daily, and follow Him. Luke 9:23— *"Then he [Jesus] said to them all: 'If anyone would come after me, he must deny himself and take up his cross daily and follow me.'"*

God, I want to follow You, but I see several things that have been holding me back. Please help me not to focus on myself, but on You. Help me not to rely on myself, but on You. Help me not to complain about the cross that I have to bear, but to have a positive attitude as I take it up daily and follow You.

Do It

A cross is an instrument of death that God uses to bring life. To follow Jesus, take up your cross daily and die to self so you'll know what real living is all about.

Day 18
Accepting Who I Am

Today's Verse

Isaiah 45:9b— *"Does the clay say to the potter, 'What are you making?'"*

Read About It

Pottery making is an ancient process in which ordinary clay can be turned into either priceless ceramics or more common vessels that serve a variety of purposes. Do you feel like priceless porcelain, useful earthenware, or a worthless cracked pot? No matter what type of vessel you are, you are not worthless. God made you carefully, with a purpose in mind. Look at how painstakingly a potter makes every piece.

First, the potter takes clay and cleans it of all small stones and pebbles. He grinds the clean clay very fine and mixes it with water. Then he strains the soupy mixture of clay and water through very fine meshes, squeezing and pressing it until it is about as thick as putty. For very fine porcelain, he must work it still further, and then he often sets it aside for several months or even years.

Then the potter fashions the clay into the shape that he has chosen. He takes a lump of clay, just large enough to make the vessel he desires, and throws it onto a revolving potter's wheel. Then he hollows out the center of the lump with his thumbs and draws and pulls at its sides with his wet hands until he has made the shape he wishes.

After vessels have been shaped, the potter dries them thoroughly in a drying room and places them in a kiln where the temperature is raised to as much 3,000° Fahrenheit. Vessels are kept at that temperature for one to three days. In the intense heat the particles of clay are fused together.

Then the potter puts a fine, glasslike glaze on the rough, porous vessels. He heats the articles again in glaze kilns. Sometimes, if more decoration is desired, the potter must fire them for a third time.

Cleaning, grinding, squeezing, shaping, heating, and heating again. The potter must do all of this to make his vessels beautiful, useful, and durable. If we looked at this from the perspective of a piece of clay, it would seem like a long process, full of needless pain. But when we look at the experienced potter hard at work, we see how lovingly and gently he handles each vessel, and we are confident that he knows what he is doing. We watch in awe as he takes a plain lump of clay and carefully turns it into a vessel designed for the exact purpose he has in mind.

Think About It

Let's think a little more about the word picture of the potter and the clay. We identified five things that the potter does to turn a lump of clay into a useful vessel.

1. Cleaning
2. Grinding
3. Squeezing
4. Shaping
5. Heating

Now let's look at Scriptures that focus on each of these actions that God takes in our lives. **In the space next to each Scripture below, place the number of the corresponding action listed above.**

___ A. Psalm 51:8b— *"Let the bones you have crushed rejoice."*

___ B. Psalm 139:13— *"For you created my inmost being; you knit me together in my mother's womb."*

___ C. 2 Corinthians 4:8a— *"We are hard pressed on every side, but not crushed."*

___ D. Malachi 3:2c— *"For he will be like a refiner's fire."*

___ E. Psalm 51:7b— *"Wash me, and I will be whiter than snow."*

Answers: A2, B4, C3, D5, E1

The metaphor of a potter and clay is often used in the Bible. Here are some of the references:

• **Romans 9:20** (NLT)— *"Who are you, a mere human being, to criticize God? Should the thing that was created say to the one who made it, 'Why have you made me like this?'"*

• **Isaiah 64:8**— *"Yet, O LORD, you are our Father. We are the clay, you are the potter; we are all the work of your hand."*

• **Isaiah 45:9** (NLT)— [God says] *"Destruction is certain for those who argue with their Creator. Does a clay pot ever argue with its maker? Does the clay dispute with the one who shapes it, saying, 'Stop, you are doing it wrong!' Does the pot exclaim, 'How clumsy can you be!'"*

• **Isaiah 45:11** (NLT)— [God says] *"This is what the LORD, the Creator and Holy One of Israel, says: 'Do you question what I do? Do you give me orders about the work of my hands?'"*

Write About It ✏

It hurts when God grinds and shapes us. Some people may think that God doesn't care about them when He lets trials wear away at them or when He allows things they had been holding onto to be taken away. Their pain may seem needless and they get angry with God for allowing it. Sometimes this causes them to distance themselves from God at the time that they need Him most. As they walk away from Him, some fall into spiritual quicksand, and they can remain stuck there permanently unless they reach out for help.

1. What are some painful ways that God is grinding and shaping you?

_____
_____
_____

2. What has been taken away that you had been holding onto? Check answers that apply to you and write specifically about your losses. Put a star next to your biggest loss:
• My dream of _____

• Security found in this person _____
or this thing _____.

• Comfort and ease from not having _____
_____.

• Other _____

3. How have you been distancing yourself from God?

_____
_____
_____
_____

4. Do you feel stuck in the spiritual quicksand of anger at God? If so, write about how you feel.

_____

_____

_____

Pray About It 🙏

Read the following prayer as you consider Today's Verse, Isaiah 45:9b— *"Does the clay say to the potter, 'What are you making?'"*

Lord, I know that I am the clay and You are the potter, and I don't have a right to question You. But in Your eyes I am much more than just clay. I am Your precious child and You invite me to come to You with all my hurts. So I humbly come to You now, Father, to tell You about things that have been upsetting me.

I don't understand why You made me as You did and why You have allowed losses and painful trials to come into my life. But I don't have to understand. I trust that You know what You're doing. And I have to cooperate with You as You make me into the vessel You designed me to be. Help me not to question You when I feel Your grinding, squeezing, and shaping. And help me not to complain when I feel that I've been in the oven too long or it is hotter than it should be in there. Instead, help me to accept these things and rejoice that You are making me into the vessel You designed me to be—beautiful in Your eyes, useful in Your plan, and durable enough to fulfill Your purpose.

Do It 👣

If you feel as worthless as a lump of clay, ask the Potter to turn you into the vessel He designed you to be.

Day 19
Defeating the Devil

Today's Verse

1 Peter 5:8— *"Be self-controlled and alert. Your enemy the devil prowls around like a roaring lion looking for someone to devour."*

Read About It

You are a terrible Christian! A silent voice screamed these condemning words at me every time I thought about how out of control my eating was. As if to confirm the message, the lady I went to for help gave me a lecture using Philippians 4:13 to hammer the point. "You can do all things through Christ...so quit overeating!" she said simply. That seemed logical enough. And my conclusion also seemed logical: Since I *should* be able to control my eating, and couldn't no matter how hard I tried, I was a terrible Christian. I didn't know it then, but I do now—my enemy the devil was prowling around like a roaring lion trying to devour me with those thoughts—just as Today's Verse warns he will do.

I often receive letters from hurting, overweight people across the country because of the books I have written about how to quit overeating. Many of these people are being devoured by the same thoughts I had. Let me share one of the letters with you. Of course, as with all of my stories, I have changed her name and any details that would reveal her identity.

Dear Julie,
I am forty years old and 200 pounds overweight. I am at the

end of my rope. I love the Lord, but feel like I am nothing but a disappointment to Him because I know I should stop overeating and I always fail. It seems the more I try to deal with this, the more I want to eat....I have diabetes and high blood pressure and a host of other problems that my doctor says are weight related....I am so down about what overeating has done to my walk with God. I just want to stay home all the time. I don't even like going to church anymore. What is there for someone like me? How do I go forward? I feel so tired and so desperate.

Mary

Do you see what the devil is doing to Mary? He is devouring her with *shoulds* and *musts*. He is making her feel so overwhelmed by her lack of power that she is forgetting about God's power, and so ashamed of her failures that she is forgetting about God's unconditional love for her. The devil is encouraging her not to pray and go to church—which are the very things that will help her. And he is delighting in telling her that she's too tired to do anything…except eat.

Think About It

Do you ever feel overwhelmed? Condemned? Confused? Helpless? These are all signs of the devil's handiwork. Today's Verse draws a vivid word picture for us: *"Your enemy the devil prowls around like a roaring lion looking for someone to devour."* Many people believe that the devil is too frightening to think about, while others believe that he's a joke—a guy in a red suit. But when we read the Bible, we realize that the devil is real and we must be prepared for his attack.

Let's look at some of the things Jesus teaches us about the devil.

• The devil can use people—even people who love us—to trip us up and distract us from the things of God. Matthew 16:23— *"Jesus turned and said to Peter, 'Get behind me, Satan! You are a stumbling block to me; you do not have in mind the things of God, but the things of men.'"*

• The devil keeps God's Word from growing in us. Mark 4:15— [Jesus said] *"Some people are like seed along the path, where the word is sown. As soon as they hear it, Satan comes and takes away the word that was sown in them."*

• We can fight the devil's lies with the truth from God's Word. Matthew 4:10— *"Jesus said to him, 'Away from me, Satan! For it is written: "Worship the Lord your God, and serve him only."'"*

Here are some other things the Bible tells us about the devil:
• He masquerades as an angel of light—2 Corinthians 11:14
• He is the accuser—Zechariah 3:1
• He is the deceiver—Revelation 12:9
• He is the father of lies—John 8:44
• He has limited power; God restrains him—Luke 22:31
• He will flee if we resist him—James 4:7
• He clouds our thinking—Matthew 13:19
• He is doomed—Matthew 25:41

When we make mistakes, God sends convicting thoughts to our minds to lead us to repentance. But the devil is a masterful deceiver; he sends accusing thoughts into our minds to lead us to shame. It is often hard to know if these thoughts are from God or the devil, but here are three ways we can tell. Under each category I'll give you examples of thoughts I had concerning my problem with overeating.

Shame from the devil

Shame is general. For example: "You're a slob. You never do anything right!"

Conviction from God

Conviction is specific. For example: "Get some help for your overeating. You're harming yourself by eating too much."

Shame comes with no plan. For example: "Get a grip; you should be able to just quit overeating."

Conviction comes with a plan. For example: "Why don't you call a Christian friend who has lost weight?"

Shame comes with no hope. For example: "You will never lose weight, so you may as well not try."

Conviction comes with hope. For example: "If you stay close to the Lord and let Him help you, one day at a time you will be able to make healthier choices."

Write About It

Place a check next to each of the following statements you have thought or said:

Things the Devil Loves to Hear Us Say

- ☐ "I am too busy to have a quiet time."
- ☐ "I know it would help me to read the Bible, but I don't do it."
- ☐ "I can't memorize Scripture well, so I don't even try."
- ☐ "I quit going to church because I don't like the minister."
- ☐ "I want to get involved in church, but don't have the time."
- ☐ "I hate myself!"
- ☐ "I know God forgives me, but I can't forgive myself."
- ☐ "I am hopeless. I never do anything right."
- ☐ "After what I've done, there is no way for God to use me."

☐ "I can't do it perfectly so I won't even try."

☐ "I'll never forgive them for what they did."

☐ "I feel so overwhelmed that I can't even think."

☐ "There's no way for me to change, even though God wants me to."

☐ "God doesn't love me because He let bad things happen to me."

☐ "I'm glad I am not as bad as she is."

☐ "All I can think about is how fat (ugly, stupid, poor) I am."

☐ "I don't want anyone to know about the *real me*, so I keep to myself."

☐ "It is my responsibility to make her happy."

☐ "I don't have time for my family because I'm so busy helping others."

☐ "I know it's wrong, but I can't help it."

Pray About It 🙏

Lord, help me to fight the devil's lies by clinging to Your truth. Help me to be self-controlled and alert so that when thoughts like ones I checked above come to mind, I can recognize that I'm under attack. And help me to use the things I learned today so that when I am in the midst of spiritual warfare, I will be victorious.

Do It 👣

Whenever you feel overwhelmed by fears, resentments, or shame, be alert because there is probably a roaring lion prowling nearby!

Day 20
Renewing My Mind

Today's Verse

Romans 12:2a— *"Do not conform any longer to the pattern of this world, but be transformed by the renewing of your mind."*

Read About It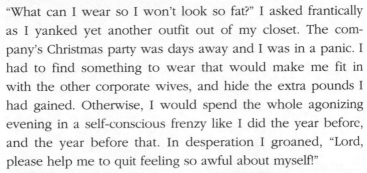

"What can I wear so I won't look so fat?" I asked frantically as I yanked yet another outfit out of my closet. The company's Christmas party was days away and I was in a panic. I had to find something to wear that would make me fit in with the other corporate wives, and hide the extra pounds I had gained. Otherwise, I would spend the whole agonizing evening in a self-conscious frenzy like I did the year before, and the year before that. In desperation I groaned, "Lord, please help me to quit feeling so awful about myself!"

God began answering my prayer almost 30 years ago as He showed me how to do the two things Today's Verse commands: 1) quit conforming to the pattern of this world, and 2) renew my mind.

One practical way I renewed my mind at the Christmas party that year was by changing my focus. When I started to feel self-conscious, instead of worrying that everyone there was looking at me, I got busy looking at everyone there— searching for someone who felt alone and self-conscious. When I went over to start a conversation with a lady in a long purple dress and an uneasy look in her eyes, my self-consciousness dissolved because my focus was on her, not on myself. That night at the party I made a life-changing discovery—God transforms me when I am willing to renew my mind by looking at my circumstances from His perspective and responding according to His Word.

Think About It

Now let's look at the first part of Today's Verse: *"Do not conform any longer to the pattern of this world."* I have had little experience with patterns, but I do recall using a pattern in Home Economics class when I made my first (and last) dress. I vowed never to sew again. I had to remove the zipper so many times that the fabric tore and I had to start over. I got a C in dressmaking, but one thing I remember is that the look and fit of the dress depended on following the pattern. If I used the wrong pattern, there was no chance that my dress would look right—even if I did put the zipper in straight. Today's Verse starts out by telling us that we are not to conform any longer to the pattern of this world. There is no way that our lives will turn out like God wants them to if we base our thoughts and actions on what the world is doing. Read this list of some of the patterns of this world.

Patterns of the World
1. Get all the gusto you can.
2. Pull yourself up by your own bootstraps.
3. Do unto others before they do unto you.
4. The one with the most toys wins.
5. Look out for number one.
6. Don't get mad; get even.

Patterns in God's Word
Place a number from the Pattern of the World (1–6 above) next to the Pattern in God's Word that opposes it.

_____A. Matthew 6:20— [Jesus said] *"But store up for your-selves treasures in heaven, where moth and rust do not destroy, and where thieves do not break in and steal."*

_____B. 1 Peter 3:9 (NLT)— *"Don't repay evil for evil. Don't*

*retaliate when people say unkind things about you.
Instead, pay them back with a blessing. That is what
God wants you to do, and he will bless you for it."*

____C. John 15:5 (NLT)— [Jesus said] *"Those who remain in
me, and I in them, will produce much fruit. For apart
from me you can do nothing."*

____D. Luke 6:31— [Jesus said] *"Do to others as you would
have them do to you."*

____E. Proverbs 25:28 (NLT)— *"A person without self-control
is as defenseless as a city with broken-down walls."*

____F. Philippians 2:4 (NLT)— *"Don't think only about your
own affairs, but be interested in others, too, and what
they are doing."*

Answers: A4, B6, C2, D3, E1, F5

Write About It

Let's look at some patterns of shame and inferiority, and
practice renewing our minds with God's Word.

Pattern of Shame and Inferiority	Patterns from God's Word
I must be a certain size or look a certain way or I will be worthless.	Psalm 116:15a (NLT)— *"The Lord's loved ones are precious to him."*
Everyone must approve of everything I say or do or I will be afraid.	Galatians 1:10 (NLT)— *"Obviously, I'm not trying to be a people pleaser! No, I am trying to please God. If I were still trying to please people, I would not be Christ's servant."*
I must fit in with the crowd or I will be a miserable misfit.	Psalm 4:3a (NLT)— *"You can be sure of this: The Lord has set apart the godly for himself."*

	2 Corinthians 5:19 (NLT)—
I must hide my mistakes under a happy Christian mask or I will be a poor testimony.	*"For God was in Christ, reconciling the world to himself, no longer counting people's sins against them. This is the wonderful message he has given us to tell others."*
I must make my loved ones happy or I will be a failure.	1 Thessalonians 4:11a— *"Make it your ambition to lead a quiet life, to mind your own business."*

When we renew a library book or driver's license, we keep the same thing that we had before, but in Today's Verse God is telling us that when we renew our minds, an exciting thing happens: We are transformed. We are no longer the same person, stuck in the same patterns.

The verb *transformed* in Greek is *metamorphoo,* from which the English word *metamorphosis* is derived. This is the word used to describe the transformation of a caterpillar to a beautiful butterfly. If you don't want to keep the same negative patterns, make a decision now to renew your mind. Then you will experience the exciting transformation that Today's Verse promises.

We renew our minds by letting God's Word, not the world, be the pattern for our thoughts and actions. If you have been following the wrong pattern and need to renew your mind, here is a practical way to change your pattern. When you're upset over something, take about 30 seconds to get away by yourself and determine to STOP following the pattern of the world:

S   **S**ee which pattern of the world is directing you. For example, you might be telling yourself, "I must fit in with the crowd or I will be miserable."

T   **T**ake that thought captive (2 Corinthians 10:5). Tell yourself, "I am not going to think that way right now."

O   **O**pen your mind to be renewed by replacing the thought you just captured with the truth from God's Word that opposes it. For example, you might tell yourself that you are set apart for God.

P   **P**raise God that you are going back to the same situation you just left, but this time you will be transformed because your mind has been renewed.

Pray About It

As you reflect on Today's verse, Romans 12:2a— *"Do not conform any longer to the pattern of this world, but be transformed by the renewing of your mind,"* tell God about the most significant negative pattern you identified and the verse that opposes it. Ask Him to transform you as you renew your mind with this verse.

Lord, I am beginning to realize where some of my negative thinking is coming from. I have been following the wrong pattern—the pattern of this world. I am going to STOP that now and start renewing my mind with Your Word. I am excited to think about the transformation that will take place when I continue to do this as I go through each day. Help me to pay attention to what I am thinking so I can recognize when I need to renew my mind. I don't want to stay like I am. I want to be transformed into the person You have designed me to be.

Do It

Don't keep on thinking what you've always thought or you will keep on getting the same results. Renew your mind with God's Word and be transformed!

Chapter 5

How Can I Become the Person I Want to Be?

Day 21

Letting God Make Me New

Today's Verse

2 Corinthians 5:17— *"Therefore, if anyone is in Christ, he is a new creation; the old has gone, the new has come!"*

Read About It

I will never read Today's Verse again without thinking of that night many years ago. My ten-year-old daughter wouldn't clean her room, so I lost my temper, screamed at her, and slammed the door as I headed to my Bible class. On the way to class, shame descended on me like a shroud because of the way I had acted.

The lesson was dry that night. Others were stifling yawns, but I was holding back the sobs that demanded to come forth. Finally, unable to suppress them, I ran to the bathroom to hide my tears. My friend Jean followed me. She hugged me as I cried. After a few minutes, still holding onto my friend, I opened my eyes and saw a glorious sight on the wall: a poster of a butterfly. On the bottom of the poster were the words: "Behold, I make all things new!"

Almost immediately I was set free from the cocoon of shame that had imprisoned me. Suddenly I knew that I was forgiven because of what Christ did for me on the cross. I felt light and almost giddy as I rejoiced in His righteousness. Though I had known the gospel message many years, that night I *experienced* His salvation. I couldn't wait to go home and apologize to my daughter.

Think About It

Have you ever had an experience when you felt the weight of your sin was instantly taken away from you? Those times are wonderful, and we long for more of them. But usually God's way of turning us into a new creation is a slow process in which, one day at a time, we learn to cooperate with Him as He changes us. Let me share with you how I cooperate with the Lord as He changes me into His new creation. I will use my absent-mindedness as an example:

1. Recognize the problem. Like many of us, I was too busy to recognize how I wasted my time. But one day I lost my glasses five or six times, my car keys twice, and an important paper I desperately needed, so I finally recognized that absent-mindedness was a big problem that I had to deal with.

2. Remain in Christ. The verse that helped me was John 15:4 (NLT) where Jesus says, *"Remain in me, and I will remain in you. For a branch cannot produce fruit if it is severed from the vine, and you cannot be fruitful apart from me."* I used to grit my teeth and try to fix my problems myself, but I learned that willpower won't work. The only way I could change was to draw close to God and cooperate with Him as He produced the change in me. I prayed about the problem and told God how it was affecting my life. Then I asked for His help and committed to pray about it every day.

3. Recall what God says. Every time I lost something, I shamed myself by saying: "Oh, you're so absentminded that you're hopeless!" I determined to stop wearing these negative labels, and instead, to see what God said about me. In 2 Timothy 1:7, I read that God gave me a sound mind (not an absent one). From then on, while I was looking for lost items, I recalled that promise and praised the Lord for the sound mind He had given me.

4. Reflect on the remedy. Some wise person said, "If you fail to plan, you plan to fail," so when I have a problem, I list several things I can do about the problem. Here is my practical remedy for absent-mindedness:

#1. List things you lose most often (answer: glasses and keys).

#2. Always put your glasses on your head when you're not wearing them. Always put your keys in your purse or on the kitchen table.

#3. In your prayer journal keep a daily list of lost items; include what you lost and where you found it. That way, you will be able to recognize trends. (This really helps, and I still keep this daily list.)

5. Rejoice in your Redeemer. A redeemer is someone who pays the price to set captives free. For example, in the days of slavery, occasionally a redeemer would come to the slave market, pay the price for slaves, and then set them free. Jesus died to free us from our old ways and to give us the ability to change. But in Galatians 5:1 we are told that with this ability comes responsibility: *"It is for freedom that Christ has set us free. Stand firm, then, and do not let yourselves be burdened again by a yoke of slavery."* As I deal with my absent-mindedness, I stand firm against excuses that would keep me stuck in my old ways. Instead, I rejoice in my Redeemer who is changing me.

Write About It

Let's review How to Become New and contrast that with How to Remain Stuck.

How to Become New	How to Remain Stuck
1. Recognize the problem.	1. Refuse to acknowledge the problem.
2. Remain in the Lord.	2. Repeat excuses.
3. Recall what God says.	3. Reject God's promises.
4. Reflect on the remedy.	4. Recite the devil's lies.
5. Rejoice in your Redeemer.	5. Report your shortcomings.

What is the most significant thing you feel stuck in?

_____

How are you remaining stuck in that old way? Pattern your answers after the five items listed above under How To Remain Stuck.

1. _____
2. _____
3. _____
4. _____
5. _____

In addition to sins and shortcomings, some of us remain stuck in negative feelings. The same five Ways to Become New will help you to overcome these feelings. Check any of these negative feelings you are stuck in and notice what God says about each.

Your Old Feelings	What God Says to You
I am depressed.	I will fill you with joy (Romans 15:13).
I am inadequate.	I will help you (2 Corinthians 9:8).
I am stupid.	I will give you wisdom (James 1:5).
I am unloved.	You are my beloved (Romans 5:8).

I am confused.	I will tell you which way to go (Psalm 32:8).
I am tired.	I will give you rest (Matthew 11:28).
I am lonely.	I am always with you (Matthew 28:20).
I am empty.	I have come that you may have a full life (John 10:10).
I am dissatisfied.	I will satisfy your desires with good things (Psalm 103:5).
I am weak.	I will strengthen you (Isaiah 41:10).
I am worthless.	You are worth a lot to me (Matthew 10:29-31).
I am worried.	I am holding your hand (Isaiah 41:13).

Pray About It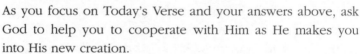

As you focus on Today's Verse and your answers above, ask God to help you to cooperate with Him as He makes you into His new creation.

God, I want to cooperate with You as You change me into the new creation that You designed me to be. Help me to remain in Christ and rely on His grace instead of my flimsy willpower. I know that I can't change myself, but I rejoice because You sent Jesus to be my Redeemer. He paid the price so that I could be free of my old sins, shortcomings, and negative feelings. Help me rejoice in my redemption and remain in Christ throughout each day so I will no longer remain stuck in my old ways.

Do It

There is an old definition of insanity: "Continuing to do the same old things, but expecting new results." Let go of the old so God can make you new!

Day 22
Understanding My Temperament

Today's Verse

Psalm 139:14a— *"I praise you because I am fearfully and wonderfully made."*

Read About It

My teacher casually handed out the graded tests, not realizing that in his hands he held the difference between life and death. I felt sure I would die if I failed another geometry test. Squeezing my eyes shut in desperate prayer, I bargained with God that if He let me pass this test, I would start paying attention in church instead of writing notes to my boyfriend. I prayed that I wouldn't get another grade of 50 like I did on the last test. Surely I had done better this time. I studied so hard. Well, I stayed up in my bedroom an hour worrying about the test and looking over some of the proofs I had copied off the board. That should count for something. I couldn't find my book, so I couldn't memorize the theorems and corollaries like I planned, but I really wanted to. "Oh God..." I started praying again, but Mr. Bedford approached with my paper in his hand. He handed me my test, and I looked down and saw...a big red 32.

After a gasp of unbelief, I moaned almost audibly, "Why, God? Why do I have to be so dumb? Why couldn't you have given me a brain like my sister's?" Linda always made A's and she hardly cracked a book. My mind swirled with this angry thought: "It just isn't fair!"

If someone had told me that day that I would graduate from college with straight A's, I never would have believed it; but when I got my RN several years later that's exactly what happened. I learned how to study—to make 3x5 cards with the questions on one side and the answers on the other, to memorize by drawing cartoons and making associations, and to take good notes and organize them neatly. I learned how to pray and rely on God to help me one day at a time. I learned how to overcome my temperament, which encouraged me to procrastinate, be forgetful, lose my books, and take sloppy notes. And I learned to quit being angry that I wasn't like others, but to do my best with what God had given me.

Think About It

When God made us, He carefully designed us with particular attributes. What we do affects these attributes and minimizes or maximizes our potential. For example, we might be born with a great ability to learn, but if we don't study and apply this ability, we will never reach our full potential. Many believe that people are also born with certain temperaments that influence how they think and act. In 400 B.C., Hippocrates decided that people have different temperaments according to their most dominant body fluid. He was wrong about the body fluid, but I believe that he was right about the four temperaments he classified.

On the next page, I have listed all four temperaments. Notice that people who are Sanguine and Choleric are extroverts who are energized by being with people, while Melancholy and Phlegmatic individuals are introverts. They may feel drained if they are around people all the time. I have listed five positive tendencies and five negative tendencies of each temperament.

TEMPERAMENTS			
Sanguine	**Choleric**	**Melancholy**	**Phlegmatic**
EXTROVERT		INTROVERT	
Outgoing	Born Leader	Analytical	Easy-going
Fun	Dynamic	Purposeful	Calm
Cheerful	Decisive	Creative	Patient
Enthusiastic	Independent	Organized	Tolerant
Optimistic	Unemotional	Conscientious	Adaptable
Needs approval	Bossy	Pessimistic	Non-assertive
Talks too much	Impatient	Moody	Indecisive
Undisciplined	Quick-tempered	Depressed	Too shy
Forgetful	Likes controversy	Low self-image	Compromising
Angers easily	Inflexible	Too introspective	Not motivated

Write About It ✐

Take this test to identify your temperament. Which answer describes you best?

1. a. I am outgoing.
   b. I have a tendency to be controlling.
   c. I am moody.
   d. I am usually easy-going.

2. a. I need the attention of others.
   b. I often make others angry.
   c. I am often critical of others.
   d. I am indecisive.

3. a. I am optimistic.
   b. I am argumentative.
   c. I am pessimistic.
   d. I am fearful.

4. a. I am friendly.
   b. I am frank.
   c. I am insecure.
   d. I am timid.

5. a. I show off.
   b. I am impatient.
   c. I am suspicious.
   d. I try to be uninvolved.

6. a. I talk too much.
   b. I work too hard.
   c. I am too easily intimidated.
   d. I am not a person of excesses.

7. a. I mix easily with others.
   b. I easily lead others.
   c. I am usually thoughtful of others.
   d. I listen to others.

8. a. I am funny.
   b. I am adventurous.
   c. I am artistic.
   d. I am contented.

9. a. I get my feelings hurt.
   b. I am proud.
   c. I sulk.
   d. I whine.

10. a. I am messy.
    b. I am cunning.
    c. I love order.
    d. I am slow.

11. a. I like to be with people.
    b. I like to delegate and direct.
    c. I like to work independently.
    d. I like to solve problems.

12. a. I'm friendly and outgoing; I want people to like me.
    b. I constantly urge my friends to do better.
    c. I'm a loner and have few friends.
    d. I'm adaptable and seem to get along with most every-
       one.

13. a. I'm lively.
    b. I'm productive.
    c. I'm analytical.
    d. I'm controlled.

14. a. I talk too much at times.
    b. I talk too loudly at times.
    c. I am bashful at times.
    d. I mumble at times.

15. a. I am undisciplined.
    b. I am bold.
    c. I am a perfectionist.
    d. I am balanced.

16. a. I want credit.
    b. I want control.
    c. I want privacy.
    d. I want routine.

17. a. I get angry frequently but am careful what I say so oth-
       ers will still like me.
    b. I get mad and let others know it.
    c. I get hurt frequently but keep it to myself.
    d. I don't get angry very often.

18. a. I am scatterbrained.
    b. I am intolerant of people who don't do things right.
    c. I feel unpopular.
    d. I am often unenthusiastic.

19. a. I lose things and forget.
    b. Others lose things and forget.
    c. I don't usually lose things or forget.
    d. I procrastinate more than I forget.

20. a. I am changeable.
    b. I am headstrong.
    c. I am resentful.
    d. I am compromising.

How to Grade the Temperament Test:
Make a mark on the appropriate line below for each of the questions in the test.
If you answered a = Sanguine _____
If you answered b = Choleric _____
If you answered c = Melancholy _____
If you answered d = Phlegmatic _____

Which was your most frequent answer?_____

Which was your second most frequent answer?_____

(Note: If they were evenly divided, you are probably Phlegmatic.) Most people have one major temperament and one minor one. If you want to do a deeper study of the temperaments, read the book *Personality Plus* by Florence Littauer.

God designed you with a purpose in mind. He made you to be unique—one of a kind. You have weaknesses, but when you look to the Lord for strength in these areas, they will remind you to lean on Him more. He will help you to overcome your weaknesses and encourage others who share them to turn to the Lord for help in overcoming theirs. God made you with strengths, but if you don't rely on Him for direction and ability, your strengths can cause misery instead of joy.

Pray About It

As you focus on Today's Verse and your answers above, ask God to help you to appreciate the temperament He gave you—to lean on Him for help with your weaknesses and rejoice in Him over your strengths.

Lord, thank You that I am fearfully and wonderfully made. I am amazed and in awe when I think about how intricately You put me together. You made me with a plan and a purpose. Help me to stop struggling against Your plan by complaining about my weaknesses, giving in to them, or feeling ashamed of them. Instead, help me to cooperate with You—rejoicing in Your wisdom and relying on Your grace. Give me the willingness to do some of the practical things I learned yesterday so that I can overcome my weaknesses with Your help. And give me the courage to use the strengths You gave me to bring glory to Your name.

Do It

Remember this: Any weakness that causes you to lean on God more is an asset.

Day 23
Letting Go of Things I Can't Change

Today's Verse

2 Chronicles 20:15b— *"Do not be afraid or discouraged because of this vast army. For the battle is not yours, but God's."*

Read About It

"Let me get this straight," I said to Lynn with a twinkle in my eye, "You're thinking about divorcing your husband because he doesn't pick up his dirty socks." Lynn replied, smiling innocently, "Well, that's not the only reason. It's just the last straw!" She continued, "Last night I got so mad when I saw them on the floor I picked up those dirty socks and threw them at him!" The petite 28-year-old who had been married for almost two years was at her wits' end. "If only I could make my husband act like he did before we got married! We used to enjoy being together and now all he wants to do after work is play pool with the guys. He seldom helps me around the house, and when I tell him what he needs to do, he just sits in his easy chair and refuses to budge."

Her husband's reaction wasn't surprising. Often when you tell people what to do, they do the opposite just to prove who's boss. Lynn and her husband were having a power struggle and both of them were losing. I have seen this many times in other marriages, but I've also seen a lot of those marriages improve miraculously when they followed the advice that someone gave me when I was a newlywed. "You cannot change anyone else," I repeated slowly, looking into Lynn's eyes to make sure she was hearing me. "You can only change yourself, but often when you change in a positive way, the other person will, also."

Waiting a few seconds to let those words sink in, I asked, "How do you treat your husband differently than you used to?" Lynn replied pensively, "Well, I used to tell him what a wonderful person he was and now, I guess...I just nag." She added, "I stopped cooking nice suppers for him. Usually I just throw something together. I used to greet him at the door with a kiss and...." She stopped in mid-sentence and I could tell that we were making progress: Lynn was beginning to see her role in the problem.

"Why don't you try a 30-day experiment?" I said. "Don't nag about his socks or things that you want him to do around the house. Instead, start cooking him nice dinners and doing other things that you used to do when you were first married." I continued, "For the next 30 days, focus on drawing closer to the Lord and letting Him change you. Let go of trying to change your husband, and let God change him." Lynn's next words were a turning point in her marriage: "I'll do it!" she said enthusiastically.

In the months that followed it was exciting to see Lynn's dying marriage being revived. Even in the first month she found that it was true: When she stopped trying to change her husband and began working on drawing closer to the Lord and letting Him change her, her husband began changing, too. He started coming home more and being more thoughtful. But things weren't perfect—they never are—and he still doesn't pick up his dirty socks. Lynn said with a laugh at our last meeting, "That doesn't matter, because now every time I pick up his dirty socks, I am reminded to pray for my husband. And I'm glad that I can do something for him that takes two seconds and helps us both to be so much happier!"

Think About It

Today's topic is letting go and letting God change the things we can't change. We can't change other people, our past mistakes, or even ourselves without God's help.

One of my favorite passages in the Bible, found in 2 Chronicles 20, tells us how to let go and let God. This is an amazing story: a massive invasion force that is sure to defeat them threatens Jehoshaphat, king of Judah. However, the prophet Jahaziel tells Jehoshaphat that God will fight this battle for him, and Jehoshaphat, rather than running away or getting his weapons ready just in case, spends his time drawing close to the Lord. He does several specific things that help him and his people to let go of things they cannot change (the vast army coming against them) and let God bring them victory. The next day God does bring them victory. He causes the invading forces to annihilate each other before Judah's army even arrives, and not one of Jehoshaphat's men is lost! Let's look to see the things that Jehoshaphat modeled for us thousands of years ago about letting go and letting God:

What You Can Do When There Is Nothing You Can Do
1. Recognize when there is a problem that you can't do anything about. 2 Chronicles 20:2a— *"Some men came and told Jehoshaphat, 'A vast army is coming against you.'"*
2. Resolve immediately to ask God what to do. 2 Chronicles 20:3a— *"Alarmed, Jehoshaphat resolved to inquire of the Lord."*
3. Get together with other believers to seek God's help. 2 Chronicles 20:4a— *"The people of Judah came together to seek help from the Lord."*
4. Remind yourself that God is sovereign—everything that happens to you passes through His fingers first. 2 Chronicles 20:6— [Jehoshaphat said] *"O Lord, God of our fathers, are you not the God who is in heaven? You rule over all the kingdoms of the nations. Power and might are in your hand, and no one can withstand you."*
5. Tell the Lord how much you need Him. 2 Chronicles 20:12b— *"We do not know what to do, but our eyes are upon you."*
6. Be still before the Lord. 2 Chronicles 20:13— *"All the*

men of Judah, with their wives and children and little ones, stood there before the LORD."

7. Don't be afraid or discouraged, thinking you have to fight God's battles for Him. 2 Chronicles 20:15b— *"Do not be afraid or discouraged because of this vast army. For the battle is not yours, but God's."*

8. Listen to people who encourage you with God's Word. 2 Chronicles 20:20— *"As they set out, Jehoshaphat stood and said, 'Listen to me, Judah and people of Jerusalem! Have faith in the LORD your God and you will be upheld; have faith in his prophets and you will be successful.'"*

9. Praise God before the victory is won. 2 Chronicles 20:21— *"Jehoshaphat appointed men to sing to the LORD and to praise him for the splendor of his holiness."*

Write About It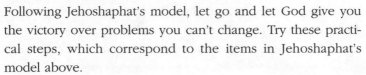

Following Jehoshaphat's model, let go and let God give you the victory over problems you can't change. Try these practical steps, which correspond to the items in Jehoshaphat's model above.

1. List problems that you can't change. Which is the most significant one?

2. Ask God what to do about it.

3. Think of someone trustworthy you can call to pray with concerning this problem. When will you call?

4. Memorize Jeremiah 32:27— *"I am the LORD, the God of all mankind. Is anything too hard for me?"*

5. Tell the Lord how much you need Him.

6. Be still before the Lord and ask Him to show you things that you can do to cooperate with Him as He brings about the victory (for example, Lynn stopped nagging). Write these things in your prayer journal.

7. Are you afraid or discouraged about the "vast army" in your life? Is it because you are trying to fight God's battles for Him? How?

8. Who encourages you with God's Word? How can you be around that person more?

9. Write a prayer praising God for victory in this situation.

Pray About It 🙏

As you pray, focus on Today's Verse.

God, thank You for Jehoshaphat's model, which teaches me what I can do when there is nothing I can do. When facing the vast army of problems that constantly seem to be attacking me, help me to quit trying to fight Your battles for You. Help me, instead, to draw closer to You and cooperate with You as You bring the victory.

Do It 👣

Stop trying to fight God's battles for Him. Let go and let God bring the victory!

Day 24
Pursuing My Vision

Today's Verse

Proverbs 29:18a *(NASB)*— *"Where there is no vision, the people are unrestrained."*

Read About It 📖

"You need to bring your recovery into the church." My vision was conceived with those simple words, and just a few months later *Step Forward* was born.

That morning, I just happened to bump into Rev. Hay in the hallway of my church, and he invited me into his office to chat. I had just joined the church and he wanted to get to know me better. "Tell me about yourself," he said casually. So I told him about my family and my nursing career and added, "I have been helping people to lose weight for the last ten years by teaching them how to draw closer to the Lord." Then I told him about how we were using the Bible and prayer to help us lose weight, and he suddenly sat up straighter, looked at me with a new intensity, and said those words that changed my life. He had a vision of how God could use me, and when he told me about it, I saw it too.

Our vision was for a ladies' Bible study with a focus on weight-loss. I couldn't wait to get started! My first class started with about 15 ladies. Soon I was teaching morning and evening classes, and before too long, other people began using my materials and leading groups in their own churches. I watched, amazed, as God began changing lives inside and out—just as He had mine. Eventually, my vision began growing in other ways and the Step Forward program was published.

As I look back on the birth and growing up of my vision for *Step Forward*, I discovered a life-changing fact: When God gives us a vision, He also faithfully provides everything necessary to make it a reality. We just have to cling to Him as we step out in faith one day at a time.

Think About It

God gives all of us many types of visions over a lifetime. Consider each of the following three types.

1. Personal—for example, breaking a bad habit, having a more intimate relationship with the Lord, or finding a mate.

2. Professional—for example, getting a new job, being a better homemaker, or getting more education.

3. Ministry—for example, helping the homeless, teaching a Bible class, or going on a missions project.

When we are walking with the Lord, He helps us to see what He wants us to do at that particular time. In Jeremiah 31:33 God says, *"I will put my law in their minds and write it on their hearts."* In other words, He gives us a vision of His will for us. Your vision may not be a large ministry, but it will be every bit as important because this is what God is calling you to do. There are three things you need for your vision to become a reality.

Confidence. Your confidence should not be in yourself—your wisdom and ability. It should not be confidence in others and the help that they can give you, or confidence in your circumstances and good fortune that may pass your way. It should be confidence in the Lord.

____1. The Lord gives you a vision of what He wants you to do.

____2. The Lord empowers you to do it.

____3. The Lord rewards you for your efforts.

Consider the following three verses and put the letter of the verse next to the corresponding action of the Lord (above).

A. Philippians 1:6— *"Being confident of this, that he who began a good work in you will carry it on to completion until the day of Christ Jesus."*

B. Matthew 25:23— [Jesus said] *"His master replied, 'Well done, good and faithful servant! You have been faithful with a few things; I will put you in charge of many things. Come and share your master's happiness!'"*

C. Proverbs 3:5–6 (NLT)— *"Trust in the LORD with all your heart; do not depend on your own understanding. Seek his will in all you do, and he will direct your paths."*

Answers: 1C, 2A, 3B

Courage. Change is challenging. There is something comfortable about the familiar—even if the familiar includes things that make you miserable. It takes courage to step out in faith and do new things that God is leading you to do. Fear may keep you stuck where you are. And sometimes people who love you may add to your fears and sabotage your efforts because they are afraid of change too. You will find the courage to step out in faith and pursue your vision if you do things that encourage you and stand guard against things that discourage you.

Here are a few of the Scriptures that helped me most when I was stepping out in faith to pursue my vision.

1. Psalm 84:11b— *"No good thing does he withhold from those whose walk is blameless."* I constantly kept this promise in mind and knew that God wouldn't withhold good things from me if I walked with Him in obedience. However, I also thought about this: If I was being careless with my thoughts, words, and deeds—walking in my own ways and doing my own thing—He would withhold the blessings I needed to see my vision become a reality.

2. Isaiah 41:13— *"For I am the LORD, your God, who takes hold of your right hand and says to you, Do not fear; I will help you."* Stepping out in faith to pursue my vision was a faith-building experience. I learned how to hold tighter to the Lord and walk closer with Him than I ever had before. Every time I felt afraid, I found the courage I needed when I remembered that the Lord was right there with me.

3. 2 Corinthians 9:8— *"And God is able to make all grace abound to you, so that in all things at all times, having all that you need, you will abound in every good work."* This is my favorite verse in the Bible! While I was pursuing my vision I clung to these wonderful promises (and still do!)—that God would always empower me to do anything that He wanted me to do. And He would always supply everything I needed, every time I needed it.

Commitment. There are many things that will try to entice you away from commitment to your vision. Two things tried to lure me away more than anything else: being too busy with other things and being overwhelmed—not knowing what to do next. I discovered practical things that helped me to remain committed to my vision. Let me share some of them with you:

1. Have a daily quiet time in which you meditate on Scriptures that help you to step out in faith, and pray about your vision as you picture it becoming a reality.

2. List things you can do to pursue your vision, and do them one at a time.

3. Meet with an accountability partner every week to discuss your progress.

4. Prioritize your time with your vision in mind.

Write About It

Answer these questions about your primary vision:

1. What is your primary vision right now?

_____

2. What are some things you can do to pursue your vision?

_____

_____

_____

3. What are you doing that might block your vision? (For example, disobeying God, not praying, making excuses, speaking negatively about your ability.)

_____

_____

_____

4. How do you waste time? How can you limit this so you will be able to pursue your vision?

_____

_____

5. Which Bible verse will you cling to as you step out in faith to pursue your vision?

_____

_____

6. Who will be your accountability partner?

_____

Pray About It 🙏

As you focus on Today's Verse and things you said in the Write About It section, pray that God will help you to pursue the vision He is giving you.

Lord, help me to see the vision You have for me, pursue it, and cooperate with You as You make it a reality. Help me not to be unrestrained, but to keep this vision in mind and rely on Your help so that I will be able to do what You have called me to do.

Do It 👣

When you think you can't, remember God can!

Day 25
Using My Gifts

Today's Verse

1 Peter 4:10— *"Each one should use whatever gift he has received to serve others, faithfully administering God's grace in its various forms."*

Read About It

I slouched down in my pew in the back of the sanctuary—trying to be as inconspicuous as possible, as if hiding would help my shame to disappear. The speaker, a missionary in Africa, was giving a glowing report of the wonderful things God was doing through her ministry, but I found it hard to listen because of all the grumbling that was going on in my mind. "You're not important like she is," the grumbler said. Then he scolded me again by saying, "You should be ashamed because you're not willing to go to Africa." I didn't understand about spiritual gifts then, but I know more now. I learned that God hasn't called me to be a missionary in Africa, so I don't need to feel guilty for not going. He has given me other spiritual gifts, and I delight in sharing them. They bring joy and fulfillment into my life when I use them while relying on God for wisdom and ability.

Today, let's look at the spiritual gifts that God has given you and explore ways you can use them to serve others and bring God glory.

Think About It

The Bible does not give us one comprehensive list of spiritual gifts. Instead, there are several lists scattered throughout the New Testament, but I believe that each Christian has one of the seven primary spiritual gifts listed in Romans 12:6–8, and may have other secondary gifts as well. Today we will focus on the seven primary spiritual gifts in Romans 12:6–8.

Seven Primary Spiritual Gifts

1. Prophecy—Proclaims God's truth to others, recognizes and exposes sin.

2. Serving—Meets the needs of others, likes to help behind the scenes.

3. Teaching—Researches and clarifies the truth from the Word for others.

4. Encouraging—Stimulates the faith of others, counsels to encourage growth.

5. Giving—Likes to share money and possessions with others.

6. Leadership—People naturally follow as this person makes goals, delegates.

7. Mercy—Shares others' burdens, empathizes with those who are in pain.

As we look at these spiritual gifts, I will answer some of the questions that people have asked me about them. Next to each question, place the letter of the Bible verse below that supports the answer.

_____1. What is the difference between a talent and a spiritual gift? A talent is a natural ability. A spiritual gift is an ability that God gives to each believer for the purpose of building up the church and bringing praise to Him through Christ.

_____2. Are some spiritual gifts unimportant? No. God gives us the spiritual gifts that He wants us to have for the exact purpose He has in mind.

_____3. How must we use our spiritual gifts? We must dish our spiritual gifts out with large helpings of spiritual fruit (love, joy, peace...).

A. 1 Corinthians 13:1–3— *"If I speak in the tongues of men and of angels, but have not love, I am only a resounding gong or a clanging cymbal. If I have the gift of prophecy and can fathom all mysteries and all knowledge, and if I have a faith that can move mountains, but have not love, I am nothing. If I give all I possess to the poor and surrender my body to the flames, but have not love, I gain nothing."*

B. 1 Corinthians 12:14–15, 18–19— *"Now the body is not made up of one part but of many. If the foot should say,*

'Because I am not a hand, I do not belong to the body,' it would not for that reason cease to be part of the body....But in fact God has arranged the parts in the body, every one of them, just as he wanted them to be. If they were all one part, where would the body be?"

C. 1 Peter 4:10–11— *"Each one should use whatever gift he has received to serve others, faithfully administering God's grace in its various forms. If anyone speaks, he should do it as one speaking the very words of God. If anyone serves, he should do it with the strength God provides, so that in all things God may be praised through Jesus Christ."*

Answers: C1, B2, A3

What are some things you need to watch out for as you use your gift?

• **Be humble.** Remember it's a gift. It didn't originate from you! Thank God for it.

• **Be appreciative.** God chose your gift especially for you and each one is important.

• **Rely on God for direction and ability.** When you don't, you may go overboard on your spiritual gift; for example, mercy can turn into rescuing and leadership can turn into bossing.

• **Don't think that just because it's easy for you, it's easy for everyone.**

• **Prioritize correctly.** For example, don't use your gifts so much that you don't have time for God or your family.

• **Don't fall into false guilt because you are not doing what someone else does.** For example, don't fret like I did about not being a missionary when God did not call you to be one.

• **Watch your spiritual fruit.** If your fruit is rotten (for example, rather than love, you have anger; rather than joy, you have fretting) you gain nothing from all of your good deeds (1 Corinthians 13:1–3).

Write About It

Take this spiritual gifts inventory. Complete the following sentences with the *best* answer:

1. I want to...
    A. Tell others when I recognize their sin.
    B. Help others when I recognize their need.
    C. Tell others the truth from the Bible.
    D. Help others to apply biblical principles.
    E. Share when I see others in need.
    F. Guide others as they do God's work.
    G. Encourage others when I see their pain.

2. I can sense...
    A. When something isn't right.
    B. When someone needs a helping hand.
    C. Details in the Bible that need reporting.
    D. Which Scripture will get someone back on track.
    E. When someone needs money.
    F. Godly goals for organizations.
    G. When others are hurting.

3. Sometimes I find myself...
    A. Correcting others who don't want my help.
    B. Helping others and sometimes neglecting my own needs.
    C. Proud of my biblical knowledge.
    D. Treating people as projects or patients.
    E. Sharing too much money.
    F. Taking over when I see inefficiency.
    G. Sympathizing when I need to be firm.

4. Too often I tend to...
    A. Be painfully direct when pointing out sins.
    B. Get involved in too many good deeds.

    C. Give Bible lessons when friends want to chat.

    D. List things my friends need to do in their walk with the Lord.

    E. Enable people to depend on me too much for financial support.

    F. Delegate work to others.

    G. Carry the burdens of others.

5. I am willing to...

    A. Suffer for doing what is right.

    B. Sacrifice my time for others.

    C. Study and learn so I can share with others.

    D. Hold others accountable to help them grow.

    E. Do without so that others can have.

    F. Spend time to help committees and organizations run effectively.

    G. Suffer with someone in pain.

6. I like to...

    A. Proclaim the truth.

    B. Give my time helping in practical ways.

    C. Share what I am learning.

    D. Encourage.

    E. Give my money.

    F. Lead.

    G. Show that I care.

7. I am critical of others who...

    A. Ignore sin.

    B. Don't help others.

    C. Don't study the Bible and share it.

    D. Don't have their quiet times.

    E. Are stingy.

    F. Don't do their job.

    G. Aren't sympathetic.

8. Nothing gives me more pleasure than...
    A. To see a sinner repent.
    B. To help someone by doing things that need to be done.
    C. To share things I have learned.
    D. To encourage someone to follow God's leading.
    E. To share what I have.
    F. To organize a large task efficiently.
    G. To just be there for someone who is sad.

9. The job I would most like to do in my church is...
    A. Evangelize.
    B. Be on the committee to help the needy.
    C. Teach Sunday school.
    D. Facilitate a support group.
    E. Help determine the budget.
    F. Be the chairperson of a large committee.
    G. Visit members in the hospital.

10. I like to...
    A. Present the gospel to a large group.
    B. Help others with their practical needs.
    C. Do Bible research.
    D. Help others solve problems.
    E. Buy things for others who have need.
    F. Determine goals, organize committees, delegate tasks.
    G. Hold someone's hand when they are going through a
       hard time.

Grading This Inventory

All of the primary spiritual gifts are represented in each question.
    A. Prophecy
    B. Serving
    C. Teaching
    D. Encouraging
    E. Giving

F. Leadership
G. Mercy

Which gift have you circled most often?

_____

How are you using your gift?

_____

_____

_____

How do you want to use your gift?

_____

_____

_____

What mistakes are you making as you use your gift?

_____

_____

_____

Pray About It

As you focus on Today's Verse, pray, dedicating your spiritual gift to God and asking Him to help you use it wisely.

God, thank You for the spiritual gift You have given me. Help me to share it generously to build up my church and bring glory to Your name. Help me not to be prideful of my gift or ashamed if I feel that it isn't as important as others' gifts.

Do It

Don't be like a spoiled child complaining at her birthday party because she didn't get the gift she wanted. Instead, appreciate the gift God has given you and let Him show you how to use it.

Chapter 6

How Can I Keep From Falling Back Into My Old Ways?

Day 26
Stumbling but Not Falling

Today's Verse

Psalm 37:24 *(NRSV)*— *"Though we stumble, we shall not fall headlong, for the Lord holds us by the hand."*

Read About It

I used to be a worrywart. When troubles swelled up before me like tidal waves, I tried to relax by imagining the Lord holding my hand, leading me to a place of safety. Many times this would help my panic to subside, but one day, no matter how hard I tried, panic kept crashing over me.

A few weeks before, we left our beautiful house in Texas and moved to South Carolina for my husband's new job. We decided to live in a furnished beach rental until we sold our old house. The rental house had a lovely view, but everything was unfamiliar and all of my friends were far away. The kids were miserable trying to adjust to their new school. And I was just as miserable trying to adjust to my new job at the hospital in town.

As I sat there on somebody else's sofa, panic began to rise up. A few tears trickled down my cheeks and an uncontrollable deluge soon joined them. I was crying too hard to pray anything except, "Help me, Jesus!" Through the torrent of muddled thoughts that followed, one clear idea kept coming into my mind: *Call the minister at the little church you went to last Sunday.* I had only been once, so I dismissed the idea. But the thought kept coming back, so I decided to call. It might be one of God's little nudges, I reasoned.

On the first ring, a pleasant sounding voice answered: "Stuart Wilson, Pawley's Island Church." I mumbled something about needing someone to talk to and he cheerfully said, "Come on over!"

I felt foolish when I entered his office. "What kind of a baby Christian is this man going to think you are?" my pride screamed in pain, and it was bruised even more when tears started to flow. But Stuart gently handed me a box of Kleenex, along with some of the popcorn he had been eating, and I told him why I had come. After listening to my story, he didn't give me a lecture about trusting the Lord. Instead, he said, "Sounds like you have a lot to worry about right now." His words erased my shame instantly, and together we formulated a plan to help me through this challenging time. That day, over popcorn and Kleenex, I learned a valuable lesson: I had pleaded for God's help, but I almost didn't take the hand He extended, because my pride tried to block the way.

Think About It

Today's Verse offers us a wonderful promise: *"Though we stumble, we shall not fall headlong, for the LORD holds us by the hand."* Have you ever helped a toddler walk? You expect him to stumble—that's what toddlers do. But because you are holding him by the hand, he won't fall and hurt himself. That is, unless he yanks his little hand out of yours and charges off on his own. When we apply the following verses to our lives, we won't stumble as often, and when we do, we will get our balance quickly because we're holding on to the Lord's hand. As you read each passage, put a star next to ones that show why you have been stumbling in your walk with the Lord.

1. Psalm 119:165— *"Great peace have they who love your law, and nothing can make them stumble."* When you love the Word of God and use it as your instruction manual, you find peace and balance in your walk with the Lord. But you will stumble if you disobey God—even in just one area—and go running off to do your own thing.

2. Proverbs 4:11–12— *"I guide you in the way of wisdom and lead you along straight paths. When you walk, your steps will not be hampered; when you run, you will not stumble."* The Lord guides you through His Word, the still small voice of His Holy Spirit, Christian counsel, your circumstances, and your feelings. You will stumble if you make decisions by considering only your feelings and circumstances.

3. Jude 24— *"To him who is able to keep you from falling and to present you before his glorious presence without fault and with great joy."* Jesus died to set you free from the power of sin and the penalty of sin. You will stumble when you excuse yourself by saying "I can't help it," or shame yourself by saying, "I can't forgive myself."

4. John 11:9b-10 (NLT)— [Jesus replied] *"As long as it is light, people can walk safely. They can see because they have the light of this world. Only at night is there danger of stumbling because there is no light."* The Bible says to bring your thoughts, words, and deeds out into the light—being open with the Lord and at least one other believer (James 5:16). You will stumble if you hide or deny your sins.

5. 1 John 2:10–11— *"Whoever loves his brother lives in the light, and there is nothing in him to make him stumble. But whoever hates his brother is in the darkness and walks around in the darkness; he does not know where he is going, because the darkness has blinded him."* You would probably never admit even to yourself that you hate someone, but if you cling to resentments without asking the Lord to help you to forgive, you will stumble.

6. Isaiah 40:30–31a— *"Even youths grow tired and weary, and young men stumble and fall; but those who hope in the* LORD *will renew their strength."* God is all-powerful. He is the one who opens and closes doors. You will stumble if you put your hope in people, things or circumstances.

The Bible also mentions stumbling blocks—things that trip us up and cause us to stumble in our walk with the Lord. Sometimes, when stumbling blocks are large enough, they can stop our journey altogether and we get stuck—unable to move forward. Here are some of the most common stumbling blocks:

Stumbling Block	What Someone Says Who Is Stumbling
1. Pride	"I don't need help." "I don't want people to know about my struggles." "How dare you say that I need to change!" "I want to do it my way."
2. Denial	"I don't have any problems." "I am too busy to be concerned about that." "It's someone else's fault." "I wonder why I can't stop overeating (shopping, etc.)."
3. Shame	"If people knew what I was really like, they wouldn't like me." "I am what I am. I can't change." I'm not as good (smart, pretty, etc.) as others."

4. Unwillingness	"I've always done it this way." "I am too busy to try something new." "I'll do it when I get around to it." "I know I can't do it, so I won't even try."

Write About It ✐

Look again at the six verses about stumbling in the Read About It section and consider your walk with the Lord during the last week. Which verse shows why you may have stumbled? What will you do so you won't continue to stumble in that area? _____

_____

_____

_____

Of the four stumbling blocks above, which one trips you up most often? What effect does it have on your walk with the Lord?

_____

_____

_____

Pray About It 🙏

As you focus on Today's Verse and the stumbling blocks of Pride, Denial, Shame, and Unwillingness, ask God to help you overcome your biggest stumbling block.

Lord, thank You for offering to take me by the hand. Help me not to yank my hand away from Yours. Instead, help me to hold tightly to You so that if I stumble, I won't fall headlong. Lead me in Your ways, guide me in Your truth, help me to love Your law and put my hope in Your Word. Help me, Lord, to knock down any stumbling blocks that are keeping me from making progress in my journey with You.

Do It

When you stumble, get right back up and thank the Lord for holding your hand.

Day 27
Giving Careful Thought to My Ways

> ## Today's Verse
>
> ***Haggai 1:7***— *"This is what the Lord Almighty says: 'Give careful thought to your ways.'"*

Read About It

One bright summer day, some friends and I went to a quiet beach to relax. While Susan and I went to play in the ocean, Linda laid out her beach towel and read a book. Susan and I had fun chatting as we took turns floating on a little raft. After a few minutes we looked up to check on Linda and were shocked to notice that she had disappeared! We looked to see if she was walking along the shore, and there was no sign of her. Then we noticed something else peculiar. The white house with the flaking paint and boarded-up windows near where Linda had been sitting was nowhere to be seen, and in its place we saw a pink house with a Snoopy banner flying over it. In an instant, it dawned on both of us what had happened: Linda wasn't the one in the wrong place—we were. Without even realizing it, we drifted so far down the beach that we completely lost sight of where we had been and where we wanted to be.

Has something similar happened to you? Have you allowed yourself to drift away from the most important things in life without even realizing it?

Think About It

I remember the morning several years ago that Today's Verse and the verses surrounding it came alive to me. A publishing house had asked me to write a book and finish it by a certain date. I worked hard writing it for six months and rushed to finish it on time. But after sending them the manuscript, I didn't hear a word from them. It had been several weeks so I didn't know if they were going to publish my book or not. That morning I was particularly frustrated, and during my quiet time I happened upon Haggai 1:5–9. The words jumped off the page at me and I felt like God was speaking to me directly through them. After each verse in this passage, I will tell you what God said to me through it.

Haggai 1:5— *"Now this is what the LORD Almighty says: 'Give careful thought to your ways.'"* When I read those words I felt that God was saying to me: Julie, I want you slow down and pay attention to what I am saying.

Haggai 1:6— *"You have planted much, but have harvested little."* You have worked hard and you are seeing few results.

"You eat, but never have enough." You're feeling dissatisfied.

"You drink, but never have your fill." You're feeling empty.

"You put on clothes, but are not warm." You have lost the warmth you once felt toward Me and the work I called you to do.

"You earn wages, only to put them in a purse with holes in it." All of your hard work seems to be for nothing.

Haggai 1:7— *"This is what the LORD Almighty says: 'Give careful thought to your ways.'"* I'm telling you again: pay attention! Stop and consider your motives for writing. Recognize things you are telling yourself and things the devil is telling you. Identify frustrations that you should be bringing to Me instead of harboring in your soul.

Haggai 1:8— *"Go up into the mountains and bring down timber and build the house, so that I may take pleasure in it and be honored,' says the LORD."* Go wherever I lead you to go and do whatever I lead you to do, but do everything with the purpose of pleasing and honoring Me.

Haggai 1:9— *"You expected much, but see, it turned out to be little. What you brought home, I blew away. Why?' declares the LORD Almighty. 'Because of my house, which remains a ruin, while each of you is busy with his own house.'"* I will withhold blessings I have in store for you until you come back to Me. Lately, you have not been writing to please Me and build up My church. You have been busy writing for your own purposes.

Today's Verses helped me realize that I had drifted away from God without knowing it. Oh, I still had my quiet times. I still prayed and studied God's Word every day. But my motives had drifted, from wanting His will to wanting my own. I spent time giving careful thought to my ways. I asked God to forgive me and then surrendered my book to Him, saying that I wanted Him to do His will with the book—not mine. As soon as I said that, I felt peace and joy that I had not experienced in a long time, and I basked in restored intimacy with the Lord. What happened next might seem contrived, but it's true: The phone rang. It was my editor calling to tell me how much they liked my new book and give me the date that it would be published.

Write About It 🖋

There are many things that may cause you to drift away from the Lord. I will mention three of them:

1. Jumbled Priorities. Pressing things drag us away from crucial things. **What are the most crucial things in your**

life? What pressing things are dragging you away from them?

Crucial Things (Eternal Significance)	Pressing Things (Immediate Significance)

2. Destructive Reasoning. Many types of destructive reasoning cause us to drift away from the Lord and His will. Here are three examples. Circle things that you have told yourself.

• **"If I can't do it perfectly, I won't do it at all."** Perfectionism causes people to trust their performance rather than the Lord. And it gives them an excuse not to try new things. Constructive reasoning says, "I can't, but God can!"

• **"I'll never _____ forever."** Whether we're saying we'll never be able to keep up a good habit or stay away from a bad one, if we have this type of destructive reasoning we will drift into hopelessness. Constructive reasoning says, "Just for today I will do the right thing whether I feel like it or not."

• **"Today doesn't count."** I was an expert with this type of reasoning. For 30 years, I said: "I've already blown my diet today, and since I'll start my new diet tomorrow, what I eat now doesn't count." Constructive reasoning says, "Each day is important. I'll take it one day at a time."

What other destructive reasoning have you identified in your life?

_____

_____

_____

3. Vicious Cycles. When your continued response to a problem makes it worse, you are caught up in a vicious cycle. Here is one of the vicious cycles I lived in: I experienced stress—so I overate—and overeating caused me to have high blood pressure, which caused more stress—so I overate to help me to deal with it. Let me help you to identify vicious cycles in your life by using this chart. I'll write my example first and then you fill in your vicious cycles.

#1 Problem	#2 Response	#3 Result	#4 Return
Stress	Overate	Blood pressure	More stress

You can stop a vicious cycle by choosing to respond to the problem in a different way. For example, I started dealing with my problems rather than eating over them. **What response do you need to change most?** _____

_____

Things like vicious cycles, destructive reasoning and jumbled priorities cause us to drift away from God and His will for our lives. We must give careful thought to our ways so we can recognize and reject these things.

Pray About It

As you consider Today's Verse, give careful thought to your ways and tell God about things that cause you to drift from Him, such as jumbled priorities, destructive reasoning and vicious cycles.

God, help me to give careful thought to my ways. Open my eyes to things that cause me to drift away from You and Your will. Give me the willingness to turn from anything that causes me to turn from You.

Do It

If you expected much and it turned out to be little, it might be because you aren't giving careful thought to your ways.

Day 28
Making Level Paths for My Feet

Today's Verse

Hebrews 12:13— *"'Make level paths for your feet,' so that the lame may not be disabled, but rather healed."*

Read About It

By applying the command in Today's Verse, I learned how to stay on track with my eating and other weaknesses, and to stop careening off the path God laid out for me. I cringe when I think about that word *careening*. It brings to mind the terrifying accident I almost had. One beautiful spring day as I was driving peacefully, but a little too fast, down the highway, the truck driver in front of me threw on his brakes. When I swerved to miss him, I lost control of my car, careened onto the bumpy, gravel-covered shoulder, and almost had a life-threatening wreck because of the unstable road I had veered onto.

I could have avoided the problem if I had planned ahead. I should have slowed down, paid more attention to the traffic, and kept a proper distance from the truck in front of me. That way I could have stayed on the smooth highway that I meant to be driving on, rather than losing control of my car on that unstable shoulder. I learned a valuable lesson that day that I have applied to many areas of my life, not just my driving. I determined to stay on track and be careful not to leave the level paths the Lord laid out for me. I do this by slowing down, planning ahead, paying attention, and being prepared. I don't do this perfectly, and sometimes I still get off track a little, but not like I used to.

Think About It 🔅

Here are ways that have helped me. Next to each I have noted when we discussed it:

How to Get on Track and Stay There
1. Have a daily quiet time in writing (Day 2).
2. Memorize and meditate on God's Word (Day 9).
3. Stand firm against the devil's lies (Day 19).
4. Meet weekly with a prayer/accountability partner (Day 24).
5. Take daily inventory (Day 27).

Before I learned how important it was to do these things consistently—even when I was "too busy"—I would get off track and not understand why. Has this happened to you? Have you succeeded in making a much-needed change and then found yourself getting off track and lapsing back into your old ways? Let's see what the Bible has to say about this.

Why Do We Get Off Track?
In Psalm 106:12–14 the psalmist tells how the Israelites were following the Lord as He led them out of slavery, but something happened to get them off track. After reading this passage, list their mistakes: *"Then they believed his promises and sang his praise. But they soon forgot what he had done and*

did not wait for his counsel. In the desert they gave in to their craving; in the wasteland they put God to the test."

1.

2.

3.

4.

**What Happens When We Stay on Track—
Following the Lord**

It takes discipline to consistently choose to walk in the ways of the Lord, but when we do, we receive wonderful blessings. In the following passage, underline four blessings given to those who make good choices: Deuteronomy 30:19b–20a— *"I have set before you life and death, blessings and curses. Now choose life, so that you and your children may live and that you may love the LORD your God, listen to his voice, and hold fast to him."*

• **We will live**—We will know vitality and serenity we've never known.

• **Our children will live**—We will be a godly influence on our children and others around us.

• **We will love the Lord**—We may think we love God, but if we are not doing what we know He wants us to do, we are not able to experience His love to the fullest.

• **We may listen to God's voice**—When we are walking in the Lord's ways, we feel His nudges, perceive His inspiration, and we are able to apply His Word to our circumstances. We don't just hear God's voice—we are able to listen to Him and do what He leads us to do.

Write About It

If you are off track, I encourage you to spend 15 minutes a day doing the things I listed under How to Get on Track and Stay There. Then I encourage you to identify the most significant thing that gets you off track, and after confessing this to the Lord, start plugging away so you can get rid of it. If you don't know where to begin, try the practical suggestions I give after each item in the following list.

What is the most significant thing that gets you off track? Check one of these or write your answer in the space provided.

1. Over-indulging (eating, spending, etc.). To begin working on the problem, identify foods or situations that get you off track and write about how it feels to be where you are. Then determine that the few minutes of pleasure from over-indulging are not worth the misery that comes with them.

2. Losing my temper. When you find yourself on bumpy ground, take time out and STOP (Day 20) before you have a wreck.

3. Wasting time. Make a list of things that you need to do. Divide them into 15-minute tasks. Write them on slips of paper, fold them, and put them in a jar. Every day pick one, and do it whether you feel like it or not. If you complete five tasks in a week, give yourself a reward.

4. Not saying *no*. When people ask you to do something, tell them you'll call them back and let them know. Pray about whether you should do it and make a pro-and-con list. Ask yourself if you will still have time to do the five things that help you to stay on track. If you won't, you probably need to say *no*.

5. Swirling thoughts. Write your thoughts in a letter to God and He will help you to identify and deal with things like anger, depression, fear, and shame that are getting you off track. If you feel stuck, reach out for help from your pastor, a trusted Christian friend, or a counselor.

6. Striving to be perfect. Perfection is an illusion that does not exist. Strive instead to rely on the Lord for help in making progress. Live by the motto "Progress, not perfection."

7. Living in regret. People who live in regret often let life pass them by. Let go of what might have been so you can cling to the blessings that God has in store for you. Start by listing the blessings that He has given you.

8. Feeling inferior and inadequate. After finishing this book, review things that you wrote and list the most significant things you learned. Start a small group using the Leader's Guide in the back and share what you learned with others.

9. People pleasing. Those who are always trying to please others live in fear. Write about what you fear. Memorize Galatians 1:10 and Isaiah 41:13.

10. Not being disciplined. Commit for one week to spend 15 minutes a day doing the things listed under How to Get on Track and Stay There. Think of something that you really want and reward yourself with it if you achieve your goal. Then make a similar commitment the following week.

What is the most significant thing that gets you off track?

_____

_____

_____

Pray About It

As you focus on Today's Verse, ask God to help you make level paths for your feet so you won't get off track. Tell Him things you commit to do that will help you to stay on track.

God, I want to follow You onto the level paths You have laid out for me. I hate getting off track. It's miserable being tossed about, out of control on a bumpy shoulder. Help me to do things we talked about today that will help me to get on track and stay there. And help me to experience the wonderful promises You give to those who choose this lifestyle of following You and Your ways.

Do It

Many of us take an average of 10,000 steps a day—115,000 miles in a lifetime. Enough to go around the planet four times! Let's stay on track so we won't waste our time wandering around.

Day 29
Practicing God's Principles

Today's Verse

Luke 6:49a— *"But the one who hears my words and does not put them into practice is like a man who built a house on the ground without a foundation."*

Read About It

"I'll never learn to write in cursives!" she said, slamming her pencil down. "I just can't do it, and never will!" My response may have seemed heartless, but I laughed as I hugged my precious eight-year-old and said, "Sarah, I'm so glad we got that out of the way. Now we can get down to work!"

When Sarah had to learn something new, she usually started by saying, "I'll never be able to do it!" She did this so often that we made a joke of it, and as she overcame one "impossible" hurdle after the next, she learned that with practice and prayer she could do almost any new task, even though at first it seemed overwhelming.

I understood Sarah's *I can't*s because I used to say that too, especially when I would read a convicting passage of Scripture and know that God was telling me to change my ways.

"I can't control my temper," I would tell Him. "I can't quit worrying!" "I can't lose weight!" Over the years I learned to laugh at my *I can't*s and get them out of the way—just like I taught my daughter to do. Then I would get busy praising God that *I can't*, but when I practice and pray, one day at a time, *He can*.

Think About It

Today's Verse tells us to put God's words into practice. In other words, practice God's principles. Here are three important points about practicing:

1. Practice makes things easier. Do you remember when you first learned to drive? Did you think you would never be able to do it? After years of practice, most of us drive without having to think much about it. Of course, we still need to pay attention, and we sometimes make mistakes, but driving seems easy most of the time. That's the way it is when we practice God's principles. At first, it seems hard, but with lots of practice, it gets easier.

2. Practice helps us learn. I took piano lessons for 12 years and I practiced almost every day. If I made a mistake, I didn't get all upset. I just went back to where I made the mistake and tried it again and again until I got it right. I found out how important it was to be consistent with my practicing. If I didn't practice for several days in a row, I found that I couldn't do what I had been able to do before.

3. Practice gives us hands-on experience. When I was getting my RN, I took microbiology, anatomy, and physiology. Each of these classes had lab courses as well as lectures so that I had hands-on experience practicing the things my professor was lecturing about. In life we have lab courses every day so that we can practice doing the things God is trying to teach us. When we look at problems as lab courses— opportunities to practice God's principles—our perspective changes and we are able to have a more positive attitude as we deal with the challenges we face.

Write About It 🖎

Let's practice some of God's principles by looking at a problem you're trying to overcome: feelings of low self-worth. First we'll look at what God's Word says, and then we'll practice these principles by looking at your lab courses.

Some of God's Principles Concerning Self-Worth

• We have great worth. God bought us at an incalculable price to Himself—the death of His Son. 1 Corinthians 6:19b–20a— *"You are not your own; you were bought at a price."*

• We are not to compare ourselves with others. 2 Corinthians 10:12— *"We do not dare to classify or compare ourselves with some who commend themselves. When they measure themselves by themselves and compare themselves with themselves, they are not wise."*

• God loves us, not because of what we do, but because of whose we are. Romans 5:8— *"But God demonstrates his own love for us in this: While we were still sinners, Christ died for us."*

• God wants us to love ourselves. Luke 10:27— *"He [Jesus] answered: 'Love the Lord your God with all your heart and with all your soul and with all your strength and with all your mind'; and, 'Love your neighbor as yourself.'"*

• We can feel good about ourselves, not when we arrive at perfection, but when we are practicing God's principles and learning from our mistakes. Paul models this principle for us. Philippians 3:12 (TLB)— *"I don't mean to say I am perfect. I haven't learned all I should even yet, but I keep working toward that day when I will finally be all that Christ saved me for and wants me to be."*

Remember: a lab course is an opportunity to practice God's principles and have hands-on experience so you can learn what God is trying to teach you.

1. Choose the verse above that speaks to you most as you deal with feelings of low self-worth.

2. What lab course are you having that helps you to practice the principle God is trying to teach you? If you can't think of one, consider the following list and then write your answer:

Sample Lab Courses

A. I have to be around someone who criticizes me frequently.
B. I keep making the same mistake even though I'm trying not to.
C. I have to do things that seem impossible to me.
D. I am so busy that I find it hard to spend time with God.
E. I feel worthless when I look at others who are doing great things.

3. Plan ahead so you can practice God's principles. Designate a lab course page in your prayer journal. On the top of the page write your lab course and the date. Then write what you will do the next time you find yourself in the "lab" working on that particular problem. Here are two examples.

Betty's Lab Course Page: My boss criticizes me frequently and makes me feel worthless. Each time my boss criticizes me, I will...

• Recognize the lab course.
• Pray silently while she is talking so I won't respond defensively.
• Remind myself of the verse I memorized about forgiveness.
• Write my boss' comments on this page when I get home.
• Tell God how I feel, ask for His wisdom about what I should do, and praise Him that my worth does not depend on what my boss says about me.
• Pray daily for my boss and my job.
• Rely on God to help me at work, one day at a time.

Joanne's Lab Course Page: I keep worrying about my children even though I'm trying not to, and this makes me feel like I'm a bad Christian. When I start worrying about my children, I will...

• Recognize the lab course and immediately say the verse I memorized about God's help.

• Write my worries on this page along with several encouraging verses so I can focus on God instead of my worries.

• Praise God that He loves me completely, despite my worries, and that my children are in His hands.

Pray About It

As you consider Today's Verse, tell God about your most difficult lab course and the principle you need to practice in the "lab."

God, thank You for being such a wonderful Teacher. I don't have to be overwhelmed with the I can'ts because You are teaching me everything I need to know. The Bible provides principles that show me how to build my faith on a firm foundation, and as I practice Your principles every day, You are helping me to become the person I have always wanted to be.

Do It

Practice doesn't make perfect, but it does make it a whole lot better. Practice God's principles today!

Day 30
Flowing with the River

Today's Verse

John 7:38 *(NLT)— "For the Scriptures declare that rivers of living water will flow from the heart of those who believe in me."*

Read About It

A few months after I became a Christian, the doctor who led me to the Lord went to a conference where he happened to meet my favorite author, Bruce Larson. When Dr. Jones told him about me, Bruce wrote me an encouraging note. I practically wore the note out reading and rereading it, but was confused about his last words to me. They said, "Don't push the River!" One afternoon a year or so later, I finally understood what that meant.

We were living in Texas at the time, and when it rains in Texas, it doesn't just dribble—it gushes! We had 24 inches of rain in less than 24 hours. When it finally quit raining, my husband and I drove around to see the results of the deluge. We stopped our car and looked at a swollen river, and the word picture Bruce Larson drew for me a year earlier came alive before my eyes. The torrent of water surged below us, vigorously overflowing the banks of what had been a quiet stream. That mighty current rushed by with such force that changing it in any way would be impossible.

I thought about Bruce's warning not to push the river and visualized myself trying to push that swirling water—to alter its course, to slow it down or speed it up—and I suddenly realized that I had been doing that very thing. All too often I complained to God about unanswered prayers—trying to push Him to do my will instead of flowing with His. While gazing down at that roaring water, I humbly confessed my arrogance, and a gentle sense of His forgiveness flowed over me.

That was 30 years ago, and every time I'm tempted to complain because God is not doing what I want Him to do, I stop and remember Bruce Larson and that swirling floodwater, and I commit once again to heed their wise message: Don't push the River.

Think About It

Jesus gives us an amazing promise in Today's Verse: rivers of living water will flow from everyone who believes in Him. We don't have to wonder about what this means because the next verse explains it: the River of Living Water is the Holy Spirit. But there are still many Christians who miss out on this Word picture because they don't understand how to live dependent on the Holy Spirit. Let's look at other verses in the Bible that tell us more about this *living water lifestyle.*

A Living Water Lifestyle

1. John 4:13-14— *"Jesus answered, 'Everyone who drinks this water will be thirsty again, but whoever drinks the water I give him will never thirst. Indeed, the water I give him will become in him a spring of water welling up to eternal life.'"* In this word picture, Jesus compares the Holy Spirit to a spring of water. The word *spring* means to leap. There are several types of springs, but all of them refer to leaping: a metal spring leaps back into place, the season spring leaps forth with blooms and blossoms, and in a bubbling spring, water leaps forth from the ground.

The moment we drink the living water Jesus offers us, we have the opportunity to lead a living water lifestyle. The Holy Spirit becomes a spring inside of us offering a perpetual source of Himself so we can begin experiencing eternal life in God's kingdom and have a taste of heaven on earth. Though we will still have problems and pain, we never again need to be drained by them. We don't have to live feeling parched and unsatisfied—we have a spring inside of us, and living water constantly leaps forth within us.

2. Psalm 1:1–3— *"Blessed is the man who does not walk in the counsel of the wicked or stand in the way of sinners or sit in the seat of mockers. But his delight is in the law of the LORD, and on his law he meditates day and night. He is like a tree planted by streams of water, which yields its fruit in season and whose leaf does not wither. Whatever he does prospers."* The word *stream* means a flowing, steady succession of water (or other liquid). This passage draws a clear picture of the stability and continuity found in people with a living water lifestyle—continually thriving, fruitful, prospering and never withering.

What a wonderful way to live, and we can choose that lifestyle when we live dependent on the Holy Spirit. The first part of this passage tells us several ways to do that:

• **Not walking in the counsel of the wicked.** In this day, we hesitate to call anyone wicked, but when you read the dictionary's definition, certain people will come to your mind. *Wicked* means "morally bad, vicious, likely to cause harm or trouble." This verse clearly warns us not to follow their advice.

• **Not standing in the way of sinners.** This command might be confusing because the Bible tells us that we are all sinners (Romans 3:23)—and we are—but when Christians confess their sins, God cleanses them from all unrighteousness (1 John 1:9). This verse exhorts us not to act like, or be best friends with, people who are not walking with the Lord. Instead, we surround ourselves with people who love God and are trying to do His will.

• **Not sitting in the seat of mockers.** A mocker is a person who ridicules others and treats them with contempt. We are called to be kind to people—even those who don't deserve it. Mockers' attitudes can be contagious, and we need to stay away from them unless our purpose for fellowship is to share Jesus with them.

• **Delighting in the law of the Lord** is another way to depend on the Holy Spirit. We love God's law because we know that heeding His commands helps us walk in God's ways and experience His blessings (Psalm 119:1), find peace and stability (Psalm 119:165), and have an intimate relationship with Jesus (John 15:10).

• **Meditating on God's law day and night** helps us depend on the Holy Spirit. As we go through each day, "What would Jesus do?" is foremost in our minds. And when we can't sleep at night, we don't count sheep; we count blessings, and recall calming verses from God's Word.

Write About It

1. Refer to John 4:13–14 as you write about this: What things do you do that leave you feeling drained? What will you do to let your spring of living water refill you so you won't run out of love, joy, peace, patience, and other spiritual fruit as you do what has to be done?

_____

_____

_____

_____

_____

2. Refer to the second passage, Psalm 1:1–3, as you write about this: Which people leave you feeling withered? How can going to your stream of living water keep you from trying to fill them from an empty bucket?

_____

_____

_____

_____

Pray About It 🙏

Pray that God will let His river of living water flow in your life.

God, I believe in You. I believe that You sent Jesus to pay for my sins. I believe that You love me unconditionally and that You are with me every minute of every day—holding Your hand out to me, calling me to Yourself. I believe that Your river of living water is inside of me to give me life and power, to satisfy my thirst, to guide and restore me. Please help me to stop damming up Your river. During the last 30 days I have identified many things that have kept me feeling worthless instead of worthy. Help me now to get this debris out of my life so that Your river can flow in me—that I might be blessed and be a blessing.

Do It 👣

Flow with the river; don't push it!

Where Do I Go from Here?

I encourage you to spend the next few days reviewing notes you have written in this book and your prayer journal. Then consider ways you can share the things you have learned with others—possibly by starting a Worthless to Worthy group in your church or neighborhood. Get together weekly with friends and use the Leader's Guide in the back of this book to help each other to keep on practicing God's principles.

Leader's Guide for Small Groups

You can start your own Worthless to Worthy group in a Sunday school class, a Bible study, a support group, or with a friend or two in your home. Here are a few guidelines for the leaders:

- The leader's guides are designed to cover five daily lessons each week, for a total of six weeks, but you may take two weeks on each chapter if you like. Class meeting times are flexible—anywhere from 30 minutes to two hours. Discuss as many of the questions as you would like each week and don't feel compelled to ask all of the questions.
- A group may consist of two to 20 people. It is, of course, possible for an individual to use the questions without being in a group, but it is much more helpful to share the answers with at least one other person.
- Emphasize the importance of confidentiality. What is said in the meetings is to stay there.
- During each discussion, take notes so that you close the meetings with specific prayers for each member. Pray for the others every day during the six weeks and ask the members to do that as well.
- Try to include all group members in the discussion, but remember they are never obligated to share.
- In order to encourage openness, instruct everyone not to give advice during the meetings. Honest sharing is encouraged when people are sure that they will not be judged or lectured.

Week 1: How Can I Accept God's Love for Me the Way I Am?

- What was the biggest thing in your childhood that caused you to have feelings of inferiority? (Day 1)
- How do you believe God may use (or has used) the biggest hurt, weakness, or mistake you listed in your "resume"? (Day 4)

- Which one of the nine qualities of God listed in Day 3 helps you most to overcome feelings of inferiority? Why?
- What new habit do you want to establish? (Day 2)
- What lies have you believed about the gospel message? (Day 1)
- When did God discipline you most? How did it help you? (Day 5)

Week 2: How Can I Experience God's Power at Work in Me?

- According to the test you took this week, are you humble or humiliated? Which of the questions that you answered "A" seems most significant? (Day 7)
- Refer to the passages about grace found in Day 8. Which one encourages you most? Why?
- What do you tend to base your worth on? (Day 10)
- In the list titled Ways to Appropriate God's Grace, which one thing do you most need to do? (Day 8) Why?
- Share a meditation on Scripture that you wrote.
- Which verse are you memorizing? Why did you choose it? (Day 9)
- Look at the chart titled What Happens When God Loves Me? Which verse do you need most to be reminded of today? (Day 10) Why?

Week 3: How Can I Leave My Unhealthy Ways Behind?

- What is the most significant symptom of shame that you are experiencing? How have you tried to cover up your shame? (Day 11)
- What are you doing that makes you feel bad about yourself? How does it hurt you? How does it "help" you? (Day 12)
- Which verse about an unforgiving person speaks to you most? As you consider the Write About It section, briefly list negative things that have happened in your life due to unforgiveness. (Day 15)

- What has been the biggest locust (regret) in your life? List ways that it caused devastation. How are you cooperating with the Lord as He restores the years the locusts have eaten? (Day 14)

Week 4: How Can I Start Doing Things Better?

- Which misconception about forgiveness have you believed? What negative effect did that have on you? (Day 16)
- When did your Potter painfully clean, grind, squeeze, shape, and heat you? What positive things happened as a result of His work? (Day 18)
- Consider the verses under Patterns in God's Word. Which one seems most significant to you, considering what you are going through right now? (Day 20)
- Which item have you believed in the list titled Misconceptions about Blessing People Who Have Been Unkind to Me? What negative effect has this had on you? (Day 16)
- Which of the practical suggestions about forgiveness helped you most? (Day 16)
- What is a cross you have had to bear? What specifically are you doing to pick up your cross daily—with a positive attitude—to follow Jesus? (Day 17)

Week 5: How Can I Become the Person I Want to Be?

- What old feeling do you feel stuck in? What does God say to you about this? What will you do to cooperate with Him so He can set you free? (Day 21)
- What is your temperament? Which of the strengths listed under your temperament is your biggest? Which of the weaknesses listed under your temperament is your biggest? (Day 22)
- What is the most significant problem that you have, over which you have no control? Choose one *new* thing you will do about it. (Day 23)
- What is your primary spiritual gift? How are you using it (or how do you hope to use it)? (Day 25)

- Have you ever felt like a new creation—suddenly released from your cocoon of shame? (Day 21)
- What is your vision for ministry (something you feel that God wants you to do sometime in the future)? Suggestion to the leader: list each vision shared and pray specifically for them at the end of the class. (Day 24)

Week 6: How Can I Keep From Falling Back into My Old Ways?

- Refer to the verses in the Think About It section in Day 26 and choose the one that shows the main reason you have been stumbling in your walk with the Lord.
- Of the four Stumbling Blocks, which trips you up most often? What are you going to do to knock this stumbling block down? (Day 26)
- What is the most significant thing that gets you off track? Refer to the list in the Write About It section of Day 28 for ideas.
- How have you changed while studying this book? How are you flowing with the River more instead of trying to push it? (Day 30)
- At the end of the class, encourage members to share what they have learned and continue their journey from worthless to worthy by rereading the book and trying different practical suggestions. Also encourage them to consider starting their own Worthless to Worthy group with other friends.

Also by Julie Morris

1-56309-754-0

Find freedom from worry by investing 15 minutes a day for 30 days. Through a daily study of the Scriptures, God's power can transform the worrying mind.

www.worrytoworship.com

Available in bookstores everywhere.

new
hope
PUBLISHERS

Inspiring Women. Changing Lives.